You and Your Newborn Baby

You and Your Newborn Baby

A Guide to the First Months after Birth

Linda Todd

THE HARVARD COMMON PRESS
Boston, Massachusetts

The Harvard Common Press
535 Albany Street
Boston, Massachusetts 02118

Printed in the United States of America

Library of Congress Cataloging-in-Publication Data
Todd, Linda.
    You and your newborn baby : a guide to the first
months after birth / Linda Todd.
        p.   cm.
    Includes bibliographical references and index.
    ISBN 1-55832-055-5
    ISBN 1-55832-054-7 (pbk.)
    1. Infants (Newborn)—Care.   2. Postnatal care.
I. Title.
RJ253.T63   1993
649'.12—dc20   92-47389

Cover art by Glenna Lang
Cover design by Joyce C. Weston
Illustrations by Susan Aldridge

10   9   8   7   6   5   4   3

To Anne Todd and Joy Peterson, who, though not parents themselves, epitomize the essential gift of motherhood, that of unconditional love. Anne, sister-in-law, soul mate, and family physician, died before her time. Her wisdom, expertise, and laugh were sorely needed, and greatly missed, many times while I completed this book. Joy, my own sister, has shared my family's life in a way that has made us all richer by far. Never was a human being more aptly named!

CONTENTS

PREFACE

In the twenty years since I became a childbirth educator, two characteristics have remained constant among the parents with whom I've worked—an eagerness to learn and a powerful desire to get their families off to a good start. These characteristics are evident in the teen mother and the couple beginning their family at age forty, in the single woman planning to raise her child on her own and in the couple in a committed relationship. This drive and devotion transcend color, religion, and ethnic origin.

In the same two decades, however, I have seen many changes in *what* women and men want to learn as they make the transition from pregnancy to parenting. Today's families insist that their childbirth preparation classes cover the time beyond birth as well as the birth itself. "What are babies like?" "How do you care for them?" "What will life be like in the first months?" "How will the baby affect our relationship?" "How will I know if the baby is well?" "What do I need to know to take care of myself after the baby is born?" are all questions now commonly heard.

Expectant parents' awareness that the baby will bring great change to their lives is blended with the fear that help will not be readily available when needed. This, indeed, is often true. New families used to look to experienced parents to guide them in the early weeks. Grandparents, aunts, and the neighbor across the backyard fence or in the apartment next door were people you could depend upon. Parenting wisdom and worries were shared informally. Today's parents often find this kind of support hard to come by.

This book was written for two reasons. First, it answers many of the practical questions parents have about the first months after a baby is born, questions about themselves and about their babies. Second, it reveals the emotional adjustment parents make as they incorporate a baby into their lives, and encourages them to build their own support networks. Each network will, of course, include some professionals, but informal sources of information and support are just as important.

The information and advice offered in this book come from many sources. Incorporated here are the insights of hundreds of parents with whom I have worked, and who have generously shared their joys and sorrows, their pride and their frustrations in the work of building families. In some cases, the information offered is based on the experience of professionals—midwives, physicians, nurses, childbirth educators, and lactation consultants. In other instances, my advice is based on scientific research, which sometimes brings clarity to matters about which new parents get a lot of conflicting advice. Finally, the advice and information offered here come from children. Two of these children are my own, who have taught me a great deal as they have moved from infancy to manhood. Many of the other children are newborn infants I have encountered in my work.

In the process of writing this book, many individuals have helped and deserve acknowledgment. Linda Ziedrich has been a tireless editor, pushing me to ensure that abstract ideas had practical application. Trish Booth, MA, ACCE, Kitty Bell, RNC, FACCE, IBCLC, Amy Lange, CNM, Janet Edwards, RN, MS, CPNA, and Kathy Thorn, RNC, MS, reviewed and commented upon the manuscript, shared their expertise, and encouraged me. Sharon and Paul Miller read the manuscript with their new daughter, Natalie, in arms. Sharon spent a morning helping me connect the written word with real life, reminding me of those things that matter to new families. Deb and Barry Todd were the first to read the manuscript, doing so as they anticipated the birth of my niece, Michaela. Their assurance that they had learned some things that would make a difference in their parenting was significant to me, especially in moments when I would have preferred doing almost anything to working on "the book." Finally, my husband, Lee, who should someday write a book on fatherhood, and my sons, Adam and Peter, who have made parenting an experience worth writing about, have been unfailing in their love and support from inception to completion of this project. No woman could ask for more than I have received from these three men.

Introduction

Regardless of whether labor is long or short, whether it is hard or easy, whether a baby is born vaginally or by cesarean, most parents recall the first hours and days after birth as crystal-clear images surrounded by haze. It is in this haze that you first take in your baby and make a giant leap from pregnancy to parenting.

Despite all the anticipatory parenting done before conception and during pregnancy, despite weeks of feeling movement within and fantasizing about your baby, despite months of having strange dreams, worrisome thoughts, and musings about what kind of parent you will be, the first time you hold your baby in your arms and call yourself mother or father, mama or papa, mommy or daddy, an awareness floods over you that life will never be the same again. Another human being is now dependent upon you for survival. More than anything else, you want to be the best parent possible. Your awareness of your baby's dependency and your desire to be a good parent will together be a great source of energy and a great source of stress. Both are part of being a parent.

Becoming a good parent means much more than knowing a lot about babies. Ask pediatric doctors or nurses what it was like for them to be new parents. They will tell you that all their knowledge about babies was not enough to keep them from being over-

1

whelmed by their own babies. All new parents feel the same way. All new parents work at knowing, understanding, and loving their babies. Your baby will work just as hard at learning to know, understand, and love you. This is the process of attachment—the work that parents and babies do together to form a deep and lasting love. It is what becoming a family is all about.

This book is written to give you some help as you make the transition from pregnancy to parenting. It offers ideas on things you can do to make this time of change easier. It is written as much to encourage as to teach you. Besides providing the information you need about taking care of yourself and your baby, it can help build your confidence in your own wisdom about your family's needs. You will find the postpartum period easier if you know what to expect during this time, if you actively participate in health-care decisions, and if you build a network of support that nurtures your growing family.

New families in the United States face some challenges that families in most other countries do not. In the United States, where nearly 99 percent of women give birth in hospitals, the average hospital stay after childbirth is two days for a woman who has given birth vaginally, three to four days for a woman who has given birth by cesarean. In many communities, new families are discharged from the hospital within twenty-four hours of birth. Such early discharge will probably become the norm by the year 2000.

In most other countries, both industrialized and developing, the postpartum period is seen as being at least as important as the prenatal period. Because of this, women giving birth in hospitals have longer stays. More importantly, services are brought to the homes of new families. No matter how long the stay in a hospital or birth center, the family's transition to home—and to sole responsibility for the newborn—is overwhelming. In many countries all new families are visited at home by midwives, nurses, or other trained personnel who teach parenting skills, assess the mother's and baby's health, and provide moral support (and sometimes, as in the Netherlands, government-paid helpers do the housekeeping!). In the United States, such services are now provided to only a small minority of women.

The Newborn Mother

How Your Body Changes and Heals after Childbirth

The first six weeks after childbirth—the postpartum or postnatal period—are a remarkable time of adjustment for all members of the new family. For the new mother, this is not only a time to learn to love and care for a new baby; it is also a time of physical recovery.

Involution of the Uterus. During the postpartum weeks your uterus, or womb, involutes, or rolls inward to its non-pregnant size and shape. During this involution, the uterus will occasionally contract. These contractions are called *afterpains* or *after-birth pains*.

Afterpains make the individual cells of the uterus smaller and shorten the uterine muscle fibers. These contractions also keep the uterus firm, thus reducing bleeding from the place where the placenta was attached to the uterine wall. Tissue in the uterus that is no longer needed breaks down and is cast off in a bloody discharge through the vagina. As old tissue is absorbed or cast off, new tissue forms over the inner wall of the uterus.

Immediately after the birth of the placenta, the top of your uterus

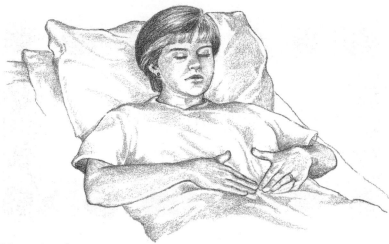

Massaging the uterus.

is just below your belly button. You can feel the top of your uterus by pressing down through the muscles in your abdomen. The uterus will feel like a large grapefruit in both size and firmness. This is how it should feel for the first two days after birth. Each day after that you will feel the uterus about one finger's breadth lower. By two weeks after the birth, your uterus will lie within the pelvis and cannot be felt through the abdominal muscles. By five or six weeks after birth, your uterus will be almost the size it was before your pregnancy.

To help your uterus remain firm after childbirth and so minimize blood loss—

• Put your baby to your breast as soon as possible after birth. The newborn's nuzzling or suckling will trigger the release of a hormone, *oxytocin*, that makes the uterus contract and stay firm. This is one of the ways in which your baby participates in your recovery while you meet your baby's need to be close to you. Even if you have given birth by cesarean, you can put your baby to breast during the first hours of recovery. A nurse can assist in positioning the baby when you feel ready.

- Massage the uterus. Occasionally during the first two hours after birth, rest one hand on your abdomen just over the uterus. If you feel your uterus soften, gently massage the top and the sides with both hands until you feel it becoming firmer. Your midwife, doctor, or nurse can show you how to do this.

   Your nurse or midwife will also check the uterus periodically. In the first two hours this may happen as often as every fifteen minutes. If the uterus has become soft, it will be massaged until it contracts. Many women find uterine massage more comfortable when they do it themselves.
- Empty your bladder often. A full bladder displaces the uterus, which makes the uterine muscles relax.

Afterpains. Although involution takes several weeks, afterpains are most noticeable in the first week after birth, especially during breastfeeding. Women having a second or subsequent baby usually say these contractions are more uncomfortable than they were after the first baby. To reduce the discomfort caused by afterpains—

- Again, keep your bladder empty. A full bladder makes afterpains worse.
- Lie on your stomach with a pillow under your lower abdomen. You may find that the contractions feel stronger when you first roll onto your abdomen, but after a couple of minutes you may experience complete pain relief.
- While you are breastfeeding, gently press against the uterus with one hand. Breathe slowly, or use the distraction or relaxation techniques that worked for you in labor.
- Discuss pain medication, if you feel you need it, with your doctor or midwife. Acetaminophen is generally considered safe to use while breastfeeding; aspirin and ibuprofen are not recommended. Sometimes stronger painkillers are prescribed. If you are breastfeeding, remind your caregiver of this and ask about the best times to take the medication in relation to feedings.

Lochia. The discharge from the vagina after childbirth, called the *lochia*, is made up of blood, tissue, and mucus from the healing uterus. You will have lochia whether you have your baby vaginally or by cesarean. To prevent infection, use sanitary pads rather than tampons to absorb the lochia. You should not use tampons or douche for at least the first six weeks after childbirth.

Lochia follow a predictable pattern of change during normal recovery. During the first few days, the discharge will be bright red. It will be heavier the first day after birth than on subsequent days. You may also notice a heavier flow when you stand up after lying down or sitting, or during breastfeeding. The discharge gradually becomes paler, and within six weeks it becomes brown, then white or yellowish. You may occasionally have red spotting, and some women have a mini-period about three weeks after birth. Generally, though, a return of bright red bleeding is a sign that you are being too active; take it as a reminder to slow down.

To increase comfort and prevent infection while there is lochia flow—

- Wash your hands before and after changing your sanitary pad.
- Change the pad every two to three hours in the first days and each time you go to the bathroom.
- Always cleanse from front to back to prevent drawing organisms in the rectal area forward to the vaginal or urinary openings.
- Use a plastic squirt bottle for cleansing the area around stitches. Fill the bottle with warm water, and spray the labia and vaginal area from front to back each time you go to the bathroom or change a pad. Pat yourself dry from front to back before putting on a clean pad.

Healing of the Cervix and Vagina. The cervix closes within hours of birth. During involution it will return nearly to its pre-pregnant size and shape.

The vagina gradually regains its tone over the months following childbirth. Almost all women say that their vaginal tissues are swollen and tender for at least the first few days after birth. If you have had an *episiotomy*—an incision made to enlarge the opening of the vagina at birth—or any tears of the vaginal opening that require stitches, the site of the stitches may be painful for a few days or a few weeks. The stitches may also feel tight, especially in the first few days. The suture used in repair of either an episiotomy or a tear is absorbed into the tissue in about ten days and does not have to be removed.

Report any of these warning signs to your doctor or midwife immediately.

Warning Signs	Possible Problems
• No lochia or scant lochia in the first two weeks after birth • Vaginal bleeding that is heavy or gushing • Large clots of blood • Soaking a pad in less than two hours	• Part of the placenta is still attached to the wall of the uterus, which could lead to hemorrhage.
• Return of bright red bleeding after lochia has become pink, brownish, or yellow	• Too much activity too soon
• Fever • Lochia that has a bad odor (normal lochia smells like menstrual flow) • Severe pain in the lower abdomen	• Uterine infection • Vaginal infection

To promote healing and reduce pain around the vaginal area—

• Place an ice pack (wrapped in a washcloth) over the perineum, the muscle between the vagina and anus, for the first few hours after birth.
• Once you are up and about, use a sitz bath, which is like a mini-tub for your bottom. Most birth facilities have sitz baths available. At home, sitting in a clean tub of warm water will be soothing. Take a sitz or warm tub bath for twenty minutes two or three times a day, or whenever the tissues begin to feel tight, for the first several days after birth.
• Alternate the warm water soaks with the use of ice packs. This technique, used in sports medicine to promote healing of dam-

aged tissue, may be more effective than sitz baths or ice packs alone. But if ice packs increase your discomfort, don't use them.

- Do pelvic floor exercises, beginning any time after birth. The pelvic floor muscles are the muscles right between your legs. Tightening and relaxing these muscles after birth increases circulation to this tender area. Tighten the pelvic floor muscles as though you were trying to stop the flow of urine. Hold the muscles tight to the count of twenty. Each time you feel the muscles beginning to relax, renew the tension until you reach the count of twenty. Repeat this exercise ten times each day.
- Tighten the pelvic floor muscles each time you get up or sit down. When you sit down, sit squarely and firmly on the most tender area. This is usually the most comfortable position.
- If your caregiver recommends it, use a spray or ointment that numbs the site of any stitches. Before applying the medication, cleanse the area with warm water and pat dry. Be cautious in using heat or cold on your perineum after applying this type of medication; since it reduces all sensation, injury could result.
- Soak sterile 4-by-4-inch gauze pads or cotton balls in witch hazel, squeeze them until they are just damp, and hold them against your stitches. (Or use commercial products containing witch hazel, such as Tucks.) Witch hazel reduces pain and swelling. You can also place witch hazel–soaked gauze pads or Tucks on your sanitary pad, which will hold the compress in place against the area of discomfort.

You can check the healing of an episiotomy or tear by holding a mirror between your legs so you can see the area around your vagina. Because the tissues are relaxed and slightly swollen in these first days after birth, it can be hard to tell what is normal and what is not normal. A nurse or midwife can show you what to look for.

Urination. You will need to urinate frequently in the first four to five days after childbirth. This is one way your body gets rid of the extra body fluid of pregnancy.

You may notice a tingling feeling when you urinate the first few times after birth. Occasionally, women have trouble urinating in the first twenty-four hours. This is because the passage of the baby through the pelvis can cause trauma to the bladder and urethra,

---

Report any of these warning signs to your doctor or midwife.

Warning Signs	Possible Problems
• Redness, swelling, or discharge from the site of a tear or episiotomy • Increasing rather than decreasing pain at the site of a tear or episiotomy • Pain in the vaginal area that persists longer than a few weeks	• Infection at the site of the episiotomy or tear • Re-opening of the incision or tear

---

which is the canal through which urine passes out of the body. The bladder and urethra may be swollen for this reason. Pressure on tissue during the baby's descent can also desensitive the urethra for the first several hours after birth. This, along with soreness around the urinary opening and the effects of medications used during labor, can depress the urge to urinate for hours after birth. If you are unaware of your need to urinate, you may retain urine during a time when your body is trying to rid itself of excess fluid.

Some very simple techniques can make urination easier. While trying to urinate—

• Run water in the bathroom.
• Have a warm drink.
• Put your hands in a basin of warm water.
• Spray warm water over your vulva.

If it is not possible to empty your bladder and it becomes distended, catheterization may be recommended. A fine, flexible tube, or catheter, is gently slipped up the urethra to the bladder. Urine then flows through the catheter until the bladder is nearly empty. Using a catheter may lead to a bladder infection, so try other methods first.

Women who give birth by cesarean have a urinary catheter put in place before surgery to keep the bladder empty. The catheter is left in place for about twenty-four hours after birth, until the woman is able to get up and go to the bathroom on her own.

Report any of these warning signs to your doctor or midwife.

Warning Signs	*Possible Problems*
• Inability to pass urine	• Trauma and swelling of the urinary tract
• A sense of an urgent need to urinate even when the bladder is empty	• Urinary tract infection
• Pain or burning while or just after passing urine	
• Pain in the lower back	
• Fever or chills	
• Blood in the urine	

Perspiration. Because of hormonal changes, most women perspire a lot in the days after birth. Perspiring a lot at night, or having "night sweats," is very common. Most women feel a need to bathe, shower, or sponge off frequently in the first days.

Bowel Movements. Most women do not have a bowel movement until the second or third day after birth. This may be because there is little to eliminate, due to normal prelabor diarrhea or fasting in labor. In addition, a natural decrease in muscle tone in the intestinal tract may persist for a number of hours after birth.

Bowel movements can also be delayed by fear. Women who have had stitches may fear that the stitches will give way if they bear down. Even women who have had no stitches often fear that "everything will come out." The first bowel movement, of course, brings relief, not disaster.

As you bear down for your first bowel movement, hold a clean sanitary pad or tissue paper firmly over your perineum. This should allay both your fear and any discomfort you feel.

To help restore normal bowel movements and promote your general recovery, eat foods high in fiber, such as fruits, vegetables, and whole grains, and drink plenty of fluids. Prune juice, in particular, stimulates bowel activity and is a good source of iron. Walking also helps.

If these things don't work and you feel constipated, talk with your doctor or midwife about using a glycerine suppository, stool softener, or enema. Laxatives are not recommended.

Hemorrhoids. Hemorrhoids, or piles, are swollen veins in the rectum. Many woman develop hemorrhoids during pregnancy, since pressure from the enlarged uterus can cause congestion in the pelvic veins. Constipation, a common problem in pregnancy, is also a cause of hemorrhoids. Sometimes hemorrhoids form during a prolonged pushing stage in labor. More commonly, hemorrhoids present before labor expand during pushing, from both the mother's bearing down and the pressure of the baby's head on pelvic-floor tissues.

Since hemorrhoids cause itching and pain, they can be a significant source of discomfort during the postpartum period. To increase your comfort—

• Prevent constipation. Drink eight to ten glasses of water each day. Eat foods high in fiber, such as bran and fresh fruit.
• Use ice packs or cold witch hazel compresses (see page 8) to reduce the swelling.
• If cold compresses don't work, use warm-water compresses or the moist heat of a sitz bath or tub bath.
• Discuss using a pain medication or stool softener with your doctor or midwife.

Breasts. *Colostrum*, the baby's first food, is present in the mother's breasts at birth. It comes in small amounts, suited to the size of the newborn's stomach. It provides complete nutrition for the newborn until the transition milk comes in, and it contains antibodies that protect the baby from many illnesses.

Colostrum also stimulates the baby to have a bowel movement. The baby's first stools are called *meconium*. This black, tarry substance contains *bilirubin*, which causes newborn jaundice. Because of its laxative effect, colostrum reduces infant jaundice (see pages 48 to 50).

After the birth of the placenta, *prolactin*, a hormone that has been present but suppressed during pregnancy, causes the milk glands in the breast to begin making milk. The level of this hormone increases as the baby suckles. If a woman does not breastfeed, the amount of prolactin will gradually decline, reaching a pre-pregnancy level by about two weeks after birth.

If you are breastfeeding . . . The more frequently you nurse your baby, the higher your level of prolactin and the more milk you produce. This makes for a wonderful system of supply and demand.

The baby's nursing also causes the release of another hormone,

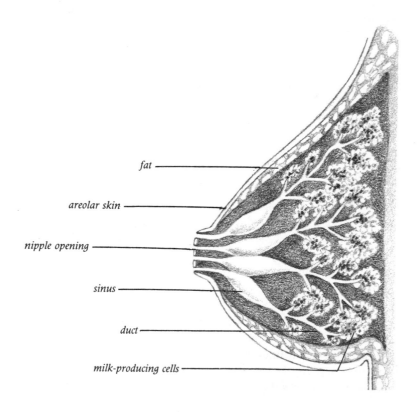

fat

areolar skin

nipple opening

sinus

duct

milk-producing cells

oxytocin. Oxytocin is responsible for what is known as the milk *letdown* or *ejection reflex.* Letdown brings the milk from the milk glands to the milk sinuses under the areola, from which the baby draws the milk out. You probably will not be aware of the letdown reflex at first. Many women say they are several days or even weeks into breastfeeding before they are aware of the full, warm, tingly feeling that usually accompanies letdown. Other signs of letdown are dripping or spraying of milk and swallowing sounds as the baby nurses. After a few days or weeks, you may feel relaxed or sleepy as the milk lets down, an effect of prolactin that can help ensure you get enough rest. This relaxed feeling is often accompanied by thirst. Have a glass of water or juice at hand every time you feed the baby.

If you have not breastfed before, you may wonder what it means for the milk to "come in." This is a process rather than a moment in time. A sign of milk coming in is heavy, enlarged, full-feeling breasts. The first milk, combined with colostrum, may appear from one to four days after birth, depending on when feeding started, how effectively the baby nurses, and your own recovery. This milk looks thin and bluish white, whereas colostrum is yellowish and thicker.

When the milk comes in, many women experience *engorgement.* In addition to your breasts feeling heavy or full, you may notice that—

- Your breasts feel warm to the touch, and firm.
- The skin on your breasts is tight, shiny, and reddish.
- The veins on your breasts are more visible than usual.
- Your breasts are tender and sore.

Engorgement is thought to be caused by both accumulation of milk and congestion of blood and lymph. Although it normally lasts only twenty-four to forty-eight hours, it is sufficiently uncomfortable that it is worth working to prevent (see page 14).

Severe engorgement can lead to a breast infection, or *mastitis.* Stress and fatique also play a role in mastitis. **Warning signs** include fever and chills, headache, general achiness, and weakness. In addition, an area of the breast becomes reddened, tender, and hard. Should you develop these symptoms, call your midwife or doctor.

WAYS TO REDUCE ENGORGEMENT AND PAIN
IF YOU ARE BREASTFEEDING

Action	Benefit
Begin breastfeeding as soon as possible after birth.	Early nursing promotes development of the newborn's suckling reflex, so the baby learns sooner how to empty the breasts.
Ask for help in positioning the baby at the breast and in assuring the baby has latched on correctly (see pages 94 to 95).	Correct positioning assures the baby milks the breast properly, thus emptying the milk sacs more completely (and also reducing your chance of sore nipples; see pages 98 to 99).
Nurse whenever the baby shows signs of hunger, such as rooting or sucking on the hands (see pages 74 to 75). Most babies are hungry every one to three hours.	Feeding in response to the baby's signals ensures a milk supply appropriate to the baby's needs.
Nurse the baby at the first breast until he or she pulls away or falls asleep. Burp the baby, then offer the other breast. Start the next feeding on that breast.	Letting the baby decide when it's time to switch sides promotes complete emptying of the breasts.
If your breasts become uncomfortably full while the baby is asleep, awaken the baby and offer the breast. You may need to change a diaper or undress the baby before nursing if the baby is very sleepy.	If the baby will take the breast, nursing will reduce the accumulation of excess milk.
Ask that the baby not be given any supplemental feedings during your hospital stay. If the baby will spend the night in a hospital nursery, ask that the baby be brought to you for feeding each time he or she awakens.	Bottle feeding can cause "nipple confusion," so the baby may have more difficulty learning to breastfeed. Supplements also reduce the baby's appetite, which means the baby may be unwilling to nurse at all when you most need relief.
As you become aware of the milk coming in, gently massage your breast while the baby suckles at it.	Massaging the breast can help the milk to flow and the milk sacs empty more completely.
If the areola is firm, express just enough milk to soften it, using your hand.	The softer areola is easier for the baby to grasp. Correct latch-on promotes better emptying of the breasts, and helps prevent sore nipples as well.
Wear a supportive bra that does not cut into skin or flatten your nipples.	The support of a good bra increases comfort.

**WAYS TO REDUCE ENGORGEMENT AND RELIEVE PAIN
IF YOU ARE BREASTFEEDING**—*Continued*

Action	*Benefit*
If you experience engorgement, apply ice packs to the breasts for ten to fifteen minutes after each feeding. (You can make an ice pack by placing a small amount of finely crushed ice in a plastic bag and wrapping the bag in a towel.)	Ice packs reduce swelling and increase comfort for many women.
If you need to, take acetaminophen or another medication recommended by your midwife or doctor as safe during breastfeeding.	Medications can relieve the pain caused by engorgement.

With prompt treatment, most women who develop a breast infection are on the way to recovery within twenty-four hours. To treat a breast infection—

- Continue nursing. Your milk will not harm your baby. If you stop nursing now, the infection may be slower to heal, and an abscess could form.
- Nurse frequently, as often as the baby is willing, and begin each feeding on the affected breast.
- Stay in bed. Your partner or another family member or friend should help care for the baby and take over other household responsibilities until you feel better.
- Place a warm, wet towel over the affected breast before each feeding.
- Drink extra fluids.
- If your midwife or doctor recommends it, take an antibiotic as prescribed (see "Thrush infection," page 99).

The risk of breast infection is not limited to the postpartum period; mastitis can occur any time while you are breastfeeding. Since it often follows overexertion, mastitis should be taken as a sign to slow down.

If you are not breastfeeding . . . In the past, women who were not planning to breastfeed were routinely given a medication to prevent milk production. Today, many doctors and midwives suggest using natural means to suppress milk production. When medication is used, the drug of choice is Parlodel. Taken in tablet form for two to three weeks after birth, Parlodel prevents secretion of prolactin. As many as 40 percent of women, however, experience engorgement or leaking of milk when they stop taking this drug. In other words, Parlodel delays milk production rather than preventing it altogether. And the drug can have side effects—dizziness, nausea, headaches, and low blood pressure.

To stop milk production without drugs, wear a supportive bra and use ice packs (see below). Do *not* express milk or apply heat to your breasts. Although these measures might bring some immediate relief from engorgement, they could also prolong the time your breasts produce milk.

Losing Weight and Eating Well. The time it takes to drop the extra pounds of pregnancy varies among women. Most women lose ten to twelve pounds at birth, then another four to five pounds over the next three to four days. After this, weight loss occurs more gradually, and depends on the way your body breaks down and uses food, what you eat, and how much you exercise. Breastfeeding women often lose weight quickly, because milk production burns calories, some of which come from fat stores. But don't forget that when you are nursing you need even more calories in your daily diet than you did when you were pregnant. As in pregnancy, it is wise to eat to appetite.

WAYS TO REDUCE ENGORGEMENT AND RELIEVE PAIN
IF YOU ARE *NOT* BREASTFEEDING

Action	Benefit
Wear a supportive bra, day and night, until about two weeks after birth.	Compressing the breast tissue inhibits milk production.
Apply ice packs to your breasts and under your arms every four hours.	Ice packs reduce swelling and relieve pain.
Take an analgesic, such as acetaminophen or ibuprofen, as recommended by your doctor or midwife.	Medications can relieve the pain caused by engorgement.

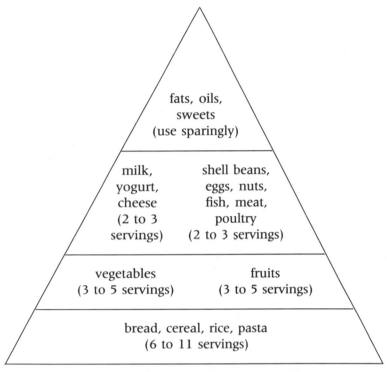

The food pyramid, a useful guide to a balanced, healthful daily diet.

A healthful diet usually includes a variety of foods from each of the food groups in the food pyramid—more from the bottom of the pyramid and less from the top. If you are breastfeeding, you'll want to be especially careful to ensure you get enough calcium— 1,600 milligrams per day—to maintain your health now and reduce the risk of osteoporosis later. If your diet is for any reason limited—for example, if it excludes milk and milk products—get advice from your doctor or midwife or a registered dietitian to ensure you're getting all the nutrients you need.

Weight-loss dieting is not recommended during breastfeeding, and it is probably a bad idea for any new mother. Taking care of a new baby demands a lot of your energy reserves, which sleep loss will deplete without the added stress of dieting.

It can be difficult for new mothers to find time to eat. You may be so busy caring for your baby that you find it has been hours since you last ate—and you are famished. To avoid this situation, stock up on healthful snack foods that you can eat on the run. Fresh fruits, carrots and celery sticks, cheeses, whole-grain crackers, and yogurt can keep you going until a meal can be prepared.

Sometimes friends, neighbors, or fellow workers get together and arrange to bring new parents meals for the first week or two after a baby is born. Experienced parents often say these meals are worth more than any gift brought to celebrate their babies' births. You might want to suggest this when friends ask if there is anything they can do to help.

In the United States, women living on limited incomes can take advantage of the WIC program (Supplemental Food Program for Women, Infants and Children). The WIC program provides coupons for free juice, milk, eggs, cheese, infant formula, and cereal products for women and children. Ask your midwife or doctor to help you register for this program, or call your local public health department for information. WIC centers also provide information about healthful eating for mothers and babies, and staff members can help in finding other health or social services in your community.

In other countries, similar food programs are usually arranged through the local visiting nurse organization or public health center.

Other Changes You May Notice. The day after birth, you may ache all over from the work you did in labor. Your arms and legs may be sore from pulling back on your legs while pushing out the baby.

Although achy legs are normal, tenderness, pain, or warmth in your calves and swollen or reddened veins are **warning signs** that you should report to your doctor or midwife immediately. These signs could indicate *thrombophlebitis*, an inflammation of a vein that can result in formation of a blood clot. Postpartum women are at slightly increased risk of this because the vein walls normally relax somewhat in pregnancy. To reduce the risk of thrombophlebitis, increase circulation in your legs by doing foot rotations (see page 21) and by getting up and walking soon after birth. Thrombophlebitis is treated with bed rest, elevation of the affected leg, hot packs, and the use of elastic stockings. Medications may also be needed to prevent infection and clot formation. The affected leg *should not* be massaged.

Joints that relaxed in pregnancy to allow for the baby's growth and birth will return to their pre-pregnancy condition within several weeks of birth. Many women, however, feel that the rib cage and pelvis remain slightly expanded for the rest of their lives.

Abdominal muscles are relaxed after birth, so the abdomen is soft and still rounded. All women have some degree of separation of the abdominal muscles, which lessens with exercise (see page 21).

Any stretch marks you have will seem more obvious after birth than before. Although stretch marks never completely disappear, they fade to silvery white lines in the months after childbirth. Darkened areas of the skin, such as the areola and the *linea nigra,* a dark line from the belly button to pubic bone, may lighten but may not completely fade.

Many women note changes in their hair after birth—most commonly, profuse hair loss. This is because pregnancy hormones stimulate hair growth. With the drop in these hormones, the extra hair that grew in pregnancy will fall out. This begins around three months after birth and usually ends within a couple of months.

Perhaps the most common feeling of new mothers after childbirth is that of being bone-tired. This seems especially true of women who have just had their first babies. Often, fatigue is combined with such excitement in the first days that sleep is difficult. The usual aches and pains of the early postpartum period can make it even harder to sleep. But beyond the first few days after birth, most women find daily naps are essential to their well-being.

Resuming Your Period. If you are breastfeeding, prolactin will suppress the production of estrogen and progesterone, which are responsible for your menstrual cycle. For this reason you will probably not have a period as long as you are breastfeeding around the clock. Reducing breastfeeding, by introducing formula or solid foods in your baby's diet, can cause a drop in prolactin levels and a return of menses.

If you are bottle feeding, your periods will probably begin within six to eight weeks of birth.

The first few periods you have after childbirth may be unpredictable. They may be shorter but more frequent than before pregnancy, or heavier or lighter than before. The menstrual cycle usually takes three to four months to regulate itself.

Since you may ovulate *before* having your first period after childbirth, you can become pregnant before then, even if you are breastfeeding. For this reason, it is important to use birth control any time you have sex after childbirth until you wish to be pregnant again. (See pages 113–16 on sexual adjustment after birth and birth control methods.)

Resuming Normal Activity and Exercise. Common sense is your best guide to resuming your normal levels of activity. A few light household tasks, a few trips up and down stairs each day, or a walk through the neighborhood may enhance your sense of well-being in the first days after birth. Signs of overexertion are increased lochia, fatigue, and achiness.

Abdominal and back muscles are weakened after pregnancy. Moderate activity and the exercises described in this section will restore your normal muscle tone. Overexertion, however, will simply weaken the muscles further.

Following are some of the exercises recommended by Elizabeth Noble in her book *Essential Exercises for the Childbearing Year* (see "Additional Reading").

The first days after birth. In the first day or two after birth, these exercises can increase your comfort and promote the return of muscle tone. Start slowly: Do each exercise two or three times at first, then gradually more.

• *Abdominal breathing and contracting*: Take a deep, relaxed breath in. As you contract the abdominal muscles, slowly exhale, blowing air out between your lips as though blowing on a trumpet. If you have had a cesarean, deep, abdominal breathing may be difficult at first. Try breathing into your upper chest first, then do mid-chest breathing. As your breathing becomes easier, take a few slow abdominal breaths. Regardless how deep your breath, contract your abdominal muscles each time you exhale.

• *Foot rotation*: While lying on your back on the bed, extend one leg and make circles with your foot. Repeat this with the other leg and foot. This exercise promotes circulation.

After the third day. You can begin these exercises after the third postpartum day if you have had a vaginal birth. If you have had a cesarean birth, your doctor or midwife will advise you regarding the best time to begin these exercises.

Before beginning the exercises, perform this check to determine the amount of separation of the *recti*, the two panels of muscle that extend down the middle of your abdomen: Lie on your back with your knees bent. Place your fingers just below your navel, as illustrated. Raise your head, moving your chin toward your chest. Press your fingertips into the abdomen to feel the two bands of abdominal muscles. If you feel a small amount of separation, one to two fingers wide, you can begin doing curl-ups. But if the separation is three to four fingers wide, do the following exercise, and put off doing curl-ups, until the separation is reduced.

• *Exercise to reduce separation of the recti muscles*: Lie on your back with your knees bent. Cross your hands over your abdomen. Breathe in deeply. Slowly exhale, and, as you do so, raise your head just off the bed, all the while pulling the abdominal muscles toward the center with your hands. Slowly lower your head to the bed.

Repeat this ten times, if possible, five times a day. Periodically check the amount of separation. Within a week, the gap should be significantly smaller.

• *Pelvic tilt*: This exercise strengthens the abdominal muscles while relieving backache. Done in an upright position, it improves posture. But it is easiest to learn when lying on your back, as follows:

Lie on your back with your knees bent. As your inhale, rock your pelvis back by pressing your lower back onto the floor. As you exhale, firmly contract your abdominal and buttock muscles, pulling your abdominal muscles in towards your back. Keep your buttocks and shoulders on the floor. Hold for three seconds, then relax.

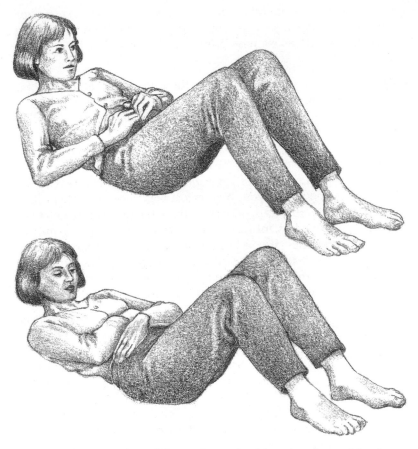

Checking for separation of the recti muscles (above) and exercising to reduce the separation (below).

Try this also while sitting or standing, or on hands and knees, as illustrated.

• *Curl-up*: This exercise restores strength in the abdominal muscles.
Lie on your back, knees bent and pelvis tilted so your lower back is against the floor. With your arms extended in front of you and your chin to your chest, roll forward as far as you can without moving your waist off the floor. Halfway up is far enough. Then slowly lower yourself to the starting position.

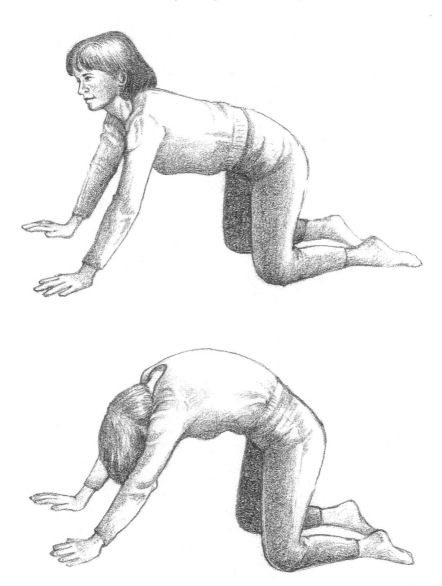

The pelvic tilt.

You can also do this exercise with your arms folded over your chest or placed behind your head. If curl-ups are too difficult, try this: Sit with your knees up, your feet on the floor. With your arms extended in front of you, lean back a little. Straighten. Gradually increase the distance you move back from your knees until you can go halfway back. As your strength increases, try the curl-up again.

Exercising at home, even if only for a few minutes each day, can be relaxing and rejuvenating. When you feel ready, you might also

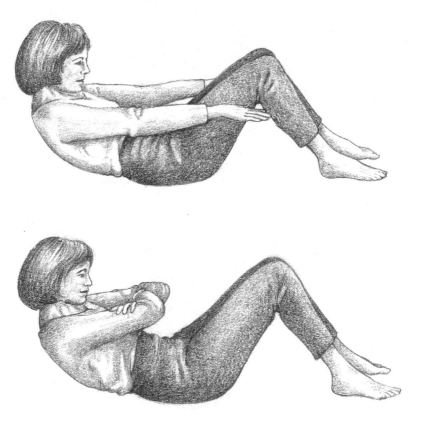

Two ways to do a curl-up.

enroll in a postpartum exercise class, for both physical conditioning and a chance to get to know other mothers. Some classes are designed for both mothers and infants, so you and your baby can "work out" together. A daily walk with the baby in a baby pack or carriage is also good for health and morale. But whatever mode of exercise you choose, be sure it is a pleasure rather than another stressful duty.

Caring for Yourself after a Cesarean. Each woman recovers in her own unique way after cesarean birth, just as after vaginal birth. Pain medications can help during the first few days (the medications given are considered safe during breastfeeding). The nurses will assist you in getting up the first time, learning to cough or huff to keep your chest clear, dealing with the gas that can follow surgery, and learning to hold your baby in ways that are comfortable for you. If assistance is not available when you need it, press your call button and ask for help.

All new parents can benefit from assistance at home after childbirth, but for a woman who has had a cesarean birth such help is essential for at least the first week. Not only are you undergoing a transformation to a nonpregnant state and learning to care for your new baby, you are recovering from major surgery. Adequate help, allowing you to rest often during the day, can make a great difference in how quickly you feel strong and well. Taking care of yourself and your baby should be your only duties until *you* feel ready to take on more.

These activity restrictions are usually recommended:

- Limit stair climbing as much as possible.
- Don't lift anything heavier than your baby for the first two weeks.
- Ask your mate or a friend to do laundry, vacuuming, and other tasks that require bending, lifting, or pushing for at least the first few weeks after birth. Then resume such work gradually.
- Do not drive a car for the first two weeks.
- Take showers instead of tub baths until the incision is completely healed and dry.

Ask your doctor or midwife for specific instructions on the care of your incision.

Report any of these warning signs to your doctor or midwife.

Warning Signs	Possible Problems
• Opening at the site of incision	• Re-opening of the incision
• Increased draining from the site of incision	• Infection of the incision
• Fever	

Take Care of Yourself! Profound physical changes, fatigue, and attending to the needs of a new baby make the postpartum period a time of great challenge. Although you will probably be healthy during these weeks, you may easily overlook warning signs because you are too tired, too busy, or too focused on your baby to seek medical care. You are important! If you notice any of the warning signs I've described, contact your midwife or doctor. If you are not sure if something is "normal," ask your caregiver.

Birth Work: Making Sense of Your Labor and Birth Experience

After a woman gives birth, her feelings about her labor are usually complex. She may feel great pride in her work of birthing—and discomfort about the way she labored. She may feel immensely grateful for the support of others and, at the same time, empty or saddened at the thought of moments when she needed more than she got from those around her. She may feel disappointed about decisions made, while feeling that those decisions were right for that moment in time. She may feel almost painfully in love with her baby, and at the same time strangely distant. These feelings do not present themselves in logical order. They wash over the new mother, skimming the surface of conscious thought in no apparent order for days after birth.

Usually, precise memory of the physical sensations of labor fades quickly. When her baby is born, a woman may be stunned by the sudden end to these powerful and painful sensations—overwhelming one minute, gone the next. She may feel disoriented in the first hours after birth.

A woman may better remember her own actions in labor than the pain or the power of the labor itself. In the days and weeks after birth, she may find herself lying awake at night or having daydreams about her labor, reliving her responses and trying to make sense of them. As pictures flash through her mind, a woman may find her heart beats faster. She may sweat, or feel weepy or anxious.

Women who have attended childbirth classes may wish that they could have been more relaxed or better at doing breathing patterns, or that they had stood and walked around more, as they may have been advised in their classes to do. Many say they had entire suitcases filled with comfort aids—pictures to gaze at, musical recordings, snacks for their companions—which never made it out of the suitcases; indeed, these things were totally forgotten in the heat of labor. Many women question decisions they made about using pain medication in labor.

A lot of women feel some disappointment in themselves when they review their labors. In their minds, they hear the sounds they made in labor—and cannot quite forgive themselves for having been so "primitive." Many recall their interactions with others—and feel a flush of embarrassment for having been less than gracious.

These moments of self-evaluation are usually accompanied by a knowledge deep within the woman that she has done something of great significance—something that seems much larger than herself. But this knowledge can be elusive.

Birth work is the work of integrating the experience of labor and birth into one's self-image. It is work done by every woman, whether her baby is born vaginally or by cesarean. Even parents who adopt a child go through birth work. For them, labor has happened in the months and years of waiting and hoping for a child. Birth work is important work—work that usually begins in the first days after birth, but that is rarely completed then. When you find yourself in the midst of this birth work, these things might help:

Storytelling. Tell your birth story to others. You may find new insights in each telling. It may be especially helpful to review the labor experience, from start to finish, with your partner. Women and their birth partners rarely have identical stories to tell. Sometimes reviewing the labor experience is like putting together a puzzle, for which each person holds some of the pieces. Partners often discover they can help each other fill in missing pieces. This review not only brings clarity to the picture, but affirms for the mother that she did well, and for the partner that his or her presence mattered. Although each person involved might assume the other knows these things, being told is of great importance.

Sometimes, after you tell your story, people may say things that seem to discount the meaning of the events described, the power of the experience, or your need for approval. A common response is "Well, the important thing is you have the baby." But the baby and the labor are two different things. In the intense moments of labor, the baby was probably far from your mind. When you review those moments, the labor itself, your own needs, and your reactions during that time are at issue, not the baby.

Writing down your birth story can also help. Many childbirth educators give families a birth report form to return after the birth. Even if no one asks for such a report, you may benefit from writing down what happened, including what labor felt like, your emotions and thoughts as it progressed, what helped and didn't help, and how you feel about the event, yourself, and those who were with you as you look back on the birth. You and your partner might each write and share your accounts.

A personal record of a baby's birth is something that you and your child will value as the years pass. Immediately after birth, you cannot imagine that you will ever forget any part of the experience. You *will* remember your labor as long as you live, but you may forget small details you'll later wish to recall.

Communicating with Caregivers. Reviewing the birth experience with your labor nurse, physician, or midwife can also help. He or she can re-explain interventions that were made, help you recall the parts of labor you only vaguely remember, and help you reconnect your responses to the physical processes occurring at the time.

You might request a copy of your labor record. This record contains sequential notes on the progress of labor and a summary of the labor and birth by your midwife or physician. The record may or may not seem to match your own recollections. Keep in mind that it reflects only a medical perspective. To the extent that it helps you understand your experience, it is useful. It is not, however, your story. You may find it useful to review the record with your doctor or midwife.

Writing a letter to your midwife or doctor, to the staff at your birth facility, or to your childbirth educator can also be useful birth work. You can tell what was particularly helpful to you, and what was not helpful. The childbirth professionals you worked with may learn a great deal from your letter, and your suggestions may even result in positive changes for other families.

Acknowledging Your Need for Support. Most women feel an immense need for support during childbirth. Part of birth work is coming to terms with how this need was met. For many women, pride in their own work is equaled only by an amazement at what others meant to them during labor.

For other women, though, some needs for support during labor may have gone unmet. This can leave a lingering pain—the pain of loneliness or even abandonment. Examining such feelings need not mean assigning blame. The truth is that labor can create needs greater than even the most loving and nurturant person can meet.

If unmet needs in labor leave you feeling resentful, discuss your feelings with those who were with you. If you can say just what would have helped and why, both you and your partner may be able to apply this insight to other events in your life.

Using Birth Videos with Care. Many women today have videotapes made of their children's births. Although these can be treasures, some words of caution might be of use. Especially in the first months after birth, watching one's own labor is a powerful experience, completely different from watching another person's. Many women find they can watch only small portions of their

videos at a time. Most women do not wish to share the videos with casual acquaintances.

Trust your feelings about viewing and sharing any video of your baby's birth. Ask others to trust and respect those feelings as well.

Accepting Your Initial Responses to Your Baby. Like her labor, a woman's initial response to her baby is something she remembers for a lifetime. Women greet their babies in as many ways as there are mothers. Before they give birth, most women anticipate a rush of loving feelings, or even tears of joy. Others anticipate instantly "feeling like a mother." Some women actually experience these things. Many do not.

Sometimes, a woman experiences a temporary holding back from the baby whose birth caused pain or emotional trauma. A new mother may have a feeling of distance—which in retrospect may seem like disinterest. Or she may feel a strong need to attend to herself; pain and exhaustion compete with interest in the baby. In retrospect, she may see herself as selfish. Coolness, distance, self-centeredness—none of these fit with any woman's conception of a "good mother." Because of this, many women say they feel guilty about their initial responses to their babies.

Many women speak of feeling outside of themselves after labor. It is as though one's personal boundaries are hazy. Is it any wonder that women feel they are not taking their babies in—"as they should?" They can hardly take themselves in! This is to be expected. Most women say it takes days to come back into themselves. This is the natural rhythm of things. Something amazing is going on. As boundaries are reclarified, they are also redefined. You *are* now a mother. Your baby is no longer one with you, as in pregnancy. But the new boundaries are extended, to connect you for a lifetime to this other person. This connection is the essential work of the first months of parenting. You may have all the loving feelings you anticipated, but if you do not, give them time to evolve, as you do the work of taking on your new role.

As a new parent, you may be surprised by the intensity of your response to your baby's appearance. Some parents describe their newborns as "perfect" or "beautiful," but just as many parents describe their newborns as red, wrinkly, or even homely in the first hours or days after birth. Few first-time parents have actually seen a brand new baby; they carry images of older infants whom they have known or seen in advertisements. Of course, advertisements rarely use pictures of newborns. No baby chosen for a commercial is going to show normal newborn blemishes such as "stork bites," peeling skin, or newborn rash.

Babies have many characteristics that bring out a nurturing response in adults. Most marked of these characteristics are the large, rounded head, the big, wide-set eyes, the rounded body, the soft skin color, the small lips, and the jerky, uncoordinated movements. These are the characteristics that make a baby "cute." They release strong, nurturant feelings in those around the baby.

But not all babies are cute at birth. For new parents, any of the baby's characteristics that seem the least bit out of the ordinary may trigger feelings of sadness, loss, guilt, anger, or anxiety. Health professionals, family members, and friends may not comprehend the power of these feelings, and so may not extend the needed support—or even recognize the feelings as valid. This leaves many parents isolated and lonely as they work through their feelings about their newborns.

If your baby's appearance does not attract you at first, share these feelings with someone you trust. Once you talk about your feelings with a sympathetic friend, you'll begin to find appealing characteristics in your baby. Our children don't need us to see them as perfect; they need us to love them for who they are and who they are becoming.

Postpartum Emotions: *"Like Nothing I've Ever Experienced Before"*

"I have never felt like this before," say many mothers in the first weeks after birth. Given the range of emotions most women experience during pregnancy, this seems hard to believe. The difference, perhaps, is that the feelings of pregnancy are centered on anticipation. The feelings of postpartum are centered on reality.

The Baby Blues. More than 50 percent of mothers experience the "baby blues," starting as early as the second day postpartum. Signs of the baby blues are feeling weepy, frustrated, disappointed, and anxious. Causes of the baby blues are not completely understood, but are probably multiple. In addition to this naturally being a very emotional time, a woman is undergoing rapid physical changes. Hormonal shifts can create a sense of being emotionally out of balance. Fatigue can contribute, too.

Most women who experience the blues say they last a day or two, or occur off and on for a couple of weeks. Being moved to tears easily can be unsettling, but it helps to accept this as normal. Letting the tears flow rather than trying to suppress them will release tension and help you feel better.

For many new mothers, postpartum emotions contain an element of grief, the natural process of recovery from a loss. You may experience a sense of loss—an emptiness—at no longer being pregnant. Although the baby in your arms may be wonderful, you may be lonely for the baby inside you.

Even a very satisfying birth experience can trigger a sense of loss. If the birth was a great "high," you may feel let down in the next few days. Knowing each birth is unique, you may feel sad that the birth of a future child won't be the same. If you do not plan to have any more children, you may feel sadness at the thought of never being pregnant again, never experiencing labor again, never caring for a newborn again. You may feel the baby is developing much too fast. Of course, you may also feel a great sense of relief that your childbearing is over, and that soon the work and worry of caring for a newborn will be a thing of the past. You may have both feelings at once.

You may also suffer grief for the loss of a hoped-for labor experience, a baby of one sex or the other, a "perfect baby," a former lifestyle, or the "old" relationship with your mate. The work involved in resolving the loss depends on its extent and its meaning in your life. Support groups, a talk with your midwife or doctor, and extra support from friends and family can all be significant in healing any loss in childbearing.

While childbearing is full of possibilities for loss, it is also full of opportunities for enrichment. It is, perhaps, the blending of these opposites with which parents must come to terms as they take on and grow in the parenting role.

Other Common Feelings. In the first days after birth new mothers commonly note a feeling of euphoria blended with anxiety. Euphoria results from a woman's having made safe passage through pregnancy and birth, and finally having the baby here. It may also come from the powerful spiritual feelings many new mothers experience. The miracle of birth can awaken a sense of creativity and a feeling of unity with mothers through the ages. Many women describe feelings of contentment—that all is natural or right with them—and a sense of being at peace, even if they are unsure about how to meet their babies' needs.

Anxiety stems from the mother's awareness of the baby's dependency and her realization that there is a lot about this job she doesn't know, regardless of any books she has read or classes she has taken or even other children she has. This anxiety is useful, in that it will probably motivate her to ask for guidance from others who have experience with this time of change.

Many new parents speak of feeling detached—as though they are living on a plane different from that of the rest of the world. This detachment is something many mothers work hard to preserve in the first weeks; they talk of "hibernating" with their newborns.

Staying home to rest and just enjoy the baby is easier when a mother has help. If your mate can arrange a leave from work to share in responsibilities at home, life will be much less stressful for everyone involved.

If you are left at home alone with a newborn, on the contrary, you may feel isolated and overwhelmed. If you are having to manage on your own, seek out a place where other new mothers gather (see pages 39–40 for suggestions). Spending time with other women and their babies will reduce your feelings of isolation and reassure you that the reason you feel overwhelmed is because your work load is very heavy—not because you are incompetent.

Many parents describe a sense of being "out of control of their lives" in the first weeks after birth. Women who have successfully managed school and career anticipate that the skills they have developed will serve them well as parents. In the long run this is probably true, but in the first weeks of parenting it is not. Newborns cannot be managed or organized. They cannot be reasoned with. They are full of needs that cannot be scheduled, needs that exist here and now and call for immediate response around the clock.

The woman who is planning a six-week or three-month maternity leave may look forward to it as a reprieve from her usual hectic life. If she has worked right up to the day of birth, she may anticipate completing many personal projects that were on hold during pregnancy. Her expectations will probably be unrealized. Even women who do not plan to return to work find their images of what life at home will be like shattered by the normal chaos of early parenthood. Those long, peaceful days spent walking the baby, organizing the household, writing lovely letters to accompany the birth announcements, or simply enjoying the baby never seem to happen. The baby cries during walks, the birth announcements are buried under piles of laundry, the house has never been messier, and *quiet* is the last word the mother would use to describe a typical day with her baby. Instead of altering their expectations, far too many women find their self-esteem heading toward an all-time low.

If this is happening to you, here are a few things that can help:

- Praise yourself for the work you are doing. First, you are going through a profound physical adjustment after childbirth—a job in itself. Second, each day you are probably spending at least five hours feeding your baby, two hours changing diapers and dressing your baby, three to five hours a day holding and comforting, and one to two hours playing with your baby. This adds up to at least eleven hours a day, before any naps, showers, eating, or plain "down time" for you. Finally, besides taking care of your baby and recovering from childbirth, you are teaching your baby about two central human emotions—trust and love. You are helping your baby to join human society, to see the world as a good and safe place in which his or her needs will be met, to feel valued and worthy of love, to find joy in being alive, and to fall in love with you. In other words, you are teaching your child not just to survive in the world, but to thrive. You are not only of critical importance to your baby, but you are helping to shape the future of humankind. All in all, you are an incredibly important person. Tell yourself that many times a day.

- Ban from your speech this sentence: "I can't seem to get anything done."
- In response to the question "What did you do today?" laugh. Or summarize all I've just said. Never, under any circumstances, say, "Nothing."

Postpartum Depression. The baby blues, some sense of loss, and the other feelings just discussed are a normal part of becoming a new parent. As powerful as they are, they are balanced by moments of joy and delight in the new baby. These moments generally compensate for the times when a mother feels anxious or overwhelmed, or is just too tired to feel much of anything.

Postpartum depression is different from the baby blues. Depression is not a normal part of emotional adjustment, but an illness with complex causes. Postpartum depression can be treated, but professional help is needed. For this reason both you and someone close to you should learn to recognize the symptoms of depression. Signs of postpartum depression are—

- Feeling sad day after day
- Unrelenting anxiety about being a parent
- Feeling unable to take care of oneself or the baby
- Lack of interest in the baby

- Feeling unable to cope
- Guilt or self-criticism about not loving or caring enough for the baby
- Continual crying
- Restlessness and insomnia, or extreme sleepiness and reluctance to get out of bed at all
- Loss of appetite and excessive weight loss
- Irritability, anger, frustration, and thoughts of harming the baby

A depressed mother may have some or all of these symptoms.

Mild to severe postpartum depression may be experienced by as many as 10 to 15 percent of women. Signs may appear any time in the first two years after childbirth.

If you are depressed, don't be afraid to seek help, for your own sake and your baby's. A baby needs a responsive mother, and a depressed woman barely has enough energy to take care of the baby's physical needs. If no one is attending to a baby's emotional and social development, the baby can become depressed as well.

Friends and family members—and even doctors—may dismiss signs of depression as normal following childbirth. If you are depressed, be persistent: ask for a referral to a mental health professional. You and your baby deserve to be well and happy.

Postpartum Psychosis. This is a rare mental illness that occurs in one in a thousand women following childbirth. It often begins within the first two weeks postpartum, frequently at the same time that women experience the normal baby blues (three to four days after birth). Signs of postpartum psychosis include seeing things or hearing voices that do not exist, insomnia, confusion, and hyperactivity. Symptoms may change over time; sometimes they seem to go away, then suddenly return. The illness can result in a woman harming herself or her baby.

Women at greatest risk for postpartum psychosis are those who have a previous history of psychosis or who have a close family member who has experienced severe mental illness. But postpartum psychosis can also occur in women without such a history.

If a mother shows signs of psychosis, she should not be left alone with the baby. Professional help is needed immediately;

hospitalization is usually required. More and more facilities are allowing women to continue caring for their babies under supervision as they recover from this illness.

Taking Care of Yourself, Physically and Emotionally

After reading about the physical and emotional changes of the first weeks after birth, you may be feeling overwhelmed. Now that you know what to expect and the warning signs to watch for, you're probably wondering what you can do to make this time more manageable. These things can speed your physical recovery and reduce your risk of postpartum depression:

Find Someone to Mother *You*. If it feels right, ask a friend or family member to stay with you for a week or two after the birth. This may be especially helpful if your pregnancy involved a lengthy period of bed rest, if you are recovering from a cesarean section, or if the baby needs special care after birth.

A family may prefer to have help the second week at home rather than the first. This gives them a few days alone to begin to get to know their baby and to start establishing a household routine before an outsider gets involved. No matter when your helper arrives, ask that person to take care of *you*—by preparing meals, shopping, doing laundry or housecleaning, and caring for any older children—so you will be able to take care of the baby.

Be selective about whom you ask to stay with you. Look for a friend or family member who you know will be sensitive to your needs and who won't increase your own workload and anxiety.

In many communities, businesses have sprung up to provide paid help to postpartum families. Paid "doulas" teach infant care, clean house, shop, prepare meals, and care for siblings. Unlike nurses, they provide comprehensive, practical help instead of medical assessment and baby care. For information about doula services in your community, consult your midwife, doctor, hospital or birth center, childbirth educator, lactation consultant, or La Leche League leader (see page 89).

Accept Offers of Help. Regardless of whether they have live-in or paid help, most new parents have friends or family members who ask, "Is there anything you need? Anything I can do to help?" Too many new parents say, "Thanks, but I can't think of anything." People love to feel needed, and certainly there is no one more deserving of help than a parent with a new baby in the house. You might instead respond to such questions by saying, "I'm so glad you offered," and follow with any of these suggestions:

- "Mealtimes are chaotic around here. It would help so much if you could bring over dinner some night."
- "I don't have time to do anything but take care of the baby. Would you be willing to come and do a couple of loads of laundry for me?"
- "My home looks like a tornado swept through it. How would you feel about coming over for a couple of hours to help me get it back in order?"
- "I feel like I've been trapped in the house for a month, even though it's only been a week. Could you come stay with the baby for an hour while I go for a walk (go shopping for something new to wear? take a long, hot bath)?"
- "My older children need a chance to get out for a while. Would you be willing to take the kids to the park for an hour?"

These are only a few suggestions. Now start your own list. Post it by your phone so you will be prepared when offers are made. Remember, the first rule of happy, healthy parenting is—ACCEPT HELP!

Limit Visitors. Helpers are one thing; visitors are another. Don't feel obliged to run an open house the first few weeks at home.

Your mate or doula can be a great help by screening phone calls and asking people to postpone visits for a couple of weeks until you feel more rested. If friends tend to drop by without calling, post a sign on your door that says, "New Family Resting. Please do not disturb."

If you want visitors, you may want to limit their time in your home. You might say, "Yes, it would be wonderful if you came by, but I'll be honest—I get tired really fast. A half-hour is about my limit."

Rest *before* You Start to Feel Tired. Don't wait until you are exhausted and weepy to rest. Sleep whenever your baby does. Unplug the phone before you lie down for a nap.

The euphoria and excitement of the first days after birth make this a hard piece of advice to follow. Don't be fooled by those feelings. When the euphoria passes, fatigue is its legacy—unless rest has been part of every day.

Don't Play Superwoman. Superwoman, you know, had no children. If she had any, "dust bunnies" would reside under her furniture, dirty dishes would be part of her kitchen decor, and a meal from the nearest fast-food joint would taste as good to her as any gourmet meal she had before the baby arrived.

Advertisements showing lovely new mothers in flowing white gowns, looking as if they just left the beauty shop, are fantasy. Real parents of real newborns usually look really tired. And they are much happier and healthier when they have their priorities in rightful order.

Since you are not Superwoman, you should not feel obliged to be nurse or counselor to friends or relatives during the early weeks after birth. Let others temporarily take over any volunteer commitments you have. Put your immediate family first during this time of transition.

Don't Move. If you can help it, do not plan a move in the first few months after your baby is born. Moving is always a big job. On top of all of the other changes taking place, a move can make it very difficult for you to settle in, rest, and focus on your new baby.

If you have to move, set realistic expectations for yourself. Unpacking every box and having your home in perfect order is something to look forward to in the future. Taking care of yourself and your baby is the priority now.

Make Friends with Other Parents. Some new parents live in neighborhoods full of other young families. If you don't, here are some ways to link up with other families:

• Arrange a reunion of your childbirth class.

- Join a postpartum support group. Your childbirth educator can refer you to one.
- Contact La Leche League, an organization that supports breastfeeding mothers. To find a local La Leche group, check your phone book or call 800-LA LECHE.
- Call your school district office and ask if the district offers early childhood education programs for parents.
- Check whether the Red Cross, the YWCA, or the YMCA offers parenting or infant CPR classes in your community.
- Join a postpartum or mother-baby exercise class at a local hospital, health club, or Y.
- Enroll in an infant massage class, and learn this comforting technique as you make new friends. A local hospital may sponsor classes; ask your childbirth educator or your baby's caregiver for information.
- Visit neighborhood parks, where parents of small children often gather.
- Strengthen relationships with colleagues from work, or other acquaintances, who have small children.
- Make inquiries in your neighborhood about play groups and babysitting co-ops.

Arrange for Child Care Early. A woman who has to return to work within weeks of her baby's birth may worry a great deal about how she will manage to turn care of her baby over to another person. She may feel depressed at the thought of having to be both wage-earner and mother, and at the thought of leaving the baby.

If your parental leave is short, make arrangements for child care as early as possible. Once you have found a care provider you trust, you can picture your baby in the safe, secure environment you have chosen.

If possible, leave the baby with the care provider once or twice before you return to work. This can give you the confidence you need that the arrangement will really work.

Even if you plan ahead and follow every suggestion on easing this time of change, there will still be tough days. Don't be hard on yourself when, despite your best efforts, things are chaotic. You will undoubtedly face moments when you wonder if you have made a big mistake in becoming a parent or in adding another child to your family. Let the feelings flow as they will. Soon you will feel much more confident, and your baby's emerging personality will pull you into a marvelous love affair.

The Newborn Baby

Health Care in the First Days

What a wonderful creation a new baby is! The adjustments the baby makes immediately after birth are amazing. The first breath inflates the lungs and triggers a permanent change in the pathway along which blood moves throughout the newborn's body. The baby's great gasp of air causes a drop in pressure in the right side of the heart and an increase in pressure in the left side of the heart. This closes the *foramen ovale*, an opening between the two sides of the heart that existed during life in the uterus. Blood rich in oxygen enters the lungs, kidneys, and liver, the work of which was done by the placenta during pregnancy. All of these marvelous changes, along with many others, occur within the first minutes after birth.

The Umbilical Cord. Within these same minutes, the doctor or midwife clamps the umbilical cord in two places. The cord is then cut between the two clamps, often by the mother's partner, with a surgical scissors. Neither mother nor baby feels anything when the umbilical cord is cut.

A small piece of the umbilical cord remains attached to the baby after cutting. It darkens, dries up, and falls off within three weeks after birth. (For information on cord care, see page 107.)

Clearing the Baby's Airway. As the baby emerges from the mother's body, the doctor or midwife wipes fluid from the baby's nose and mouth. A rubber bulb syringe may also be used to clear fluid from the mouth and nose. This reduces the chance that the baby might inhale fluid into the lungs.

Occasionally, an instrument called a mucus trap is used, immediately after the head emerges, or in the first moments after birth. A long, thin plastic tube is inserted down the baby's throat to clear mucus from around the vocal cords. The mucus trap is most commonly used when the mother's amniotic fluid is colored with meconium, indicating the baby has had a bowel movement while still in the uterus. Suctioning reduces the risk of the baby's breathing in this stained fluid, which could cause pneumonia.

If a baby's breathing is irregular, oxygen may be given through a mask placed over the baby's nose and mouth.

The Apgar Scores. A newborn is given exams at one and five minutes after birth, so quickly that you may not notice their taking place. Their results are the baby's Apgar scores. The doctor, midwife, or nurse checks the baby's heart rate, breathing effort, muscle tone, reflex response, and color, scoring each at 0 to 2 points, for a maximum score of 10. A score of 7 or above means the baby is in good condition; a lower score may mean the baby needs assistance with breathing, or other special treatment.

Helping the Baby Stay Warm. For the full-term baby who is well at birth, the primary need is to keep warm. Immediately after birth, the baby is dried off. He or she may be wrapped in warm blankets or held naked against the mother's skin, with a warm blanket covering both. The mother's body heat warms the baby as effectively as a radiant heat panel, which some hospitals use.

The Newborn's Alert State. Babies are born ready to interact with the world. In the first few hours after birth, your baby will probably be quiet and alert. When held, your baby will look into your eyes,

mold his or her body to fit snuggly in your arms, and respond to your voice. When your baby hears your voice, he or she will turn to look for you. Infants at birth show a clear preference for the voices they have heard often during prenatal life—those of parents, siblings, or other people who share the home.

You can help your baby get to know you by making the room as peaceful as possible. Dim the lights, close the curtains or blinds, and reduce any noise in the room while you hold your baby. Then the baby can focus on you, listen to your voice, and enjoy your touch.

Newborn Procedures and Tests. The procedures and tests described on pages 46 to 47 are done as part of newborn care in most hospitals and birth centers. Some of the procedures are required by state or provincial law. Whether a test or procedure is done because of a law or simply as hospital routine, you have the right to an explanation of its benefits and risks. If you object to the procedure, discuss any choice you may have with your doctor, midwife, or nurse. You may have the right to refuse the treatment, but you may also be required to sign a form that says you have refused it.

The First Bath. In hospitals, newborns are given the first bath and shampoo within the first several hours after birth. There is no rush. Parents may prefer to bathe the baby themselves or have the bath done at their bedside rather than in a hospital nursery. Let your midwife, doctor, or nurse know your preferences.

The First Weighing and Measuring. Newborns are usually weighed, and measured for length and head circumference, within the first few hours after birth. This provides baseline figures for monitoring the baby's growth at well-baby checkups. Newborns commonly lose 10 percent of their birth weight in the first two days after birth, but this weight is usually regained within ten days.

The Exam for Gestational Age. Within eight hours of birth, your baby will probably be examined to determine his or her maturity. The nurse will examine the baby's reflexes, muscle tone, posture, neurologic responses, and other signs of physical maturity. Results of this exam are compared with the baby's weight, length, and head circumference. A baby who is small relative to his or her neurological development is said to be "small for gestational age." One who is large relative to this development is said to be "large for gestational age." A baby who is at an expected size for neurological development is said to be "appropriate for gestational age." Knowing the baby's gestational age can help parents understand their newborn's abilities and behavior.

The First Physical Exams. A baby normally has the first complete physical exam within twenty-four hours of birth. This exam may be done by the baby's caregiver or by a doctor who works at the birth facility. A second, less comprehensive physical exam is usually done before the baby is discharged from a hospital or birth center.

Either or both of these exams can be done at your bedside, or you

NEWBORN PROCEDURES AND TESTS

Procedure or Test	What Is It?	Why Is It Done?	Comments
Eye treatment	Antibiotic ointment (erythromycin or tetracycline) or silver nitrate drops are placed in the eyes of the newborn.	The medication prevents infection of the baby's eyes with gonorrhea, chlamydia, or pneumococcal bacteria, to which the baby is exposed at birth if the mother is infected. Without eye treatment, infants exposed to gonorrhea can develop blindness.	Treatment of all newborns is required by law in most states and provinces. Both the antibiotic ointment and the silver nitrate drops blur the baby's vision for a short time. Silver nitrate is also irritating to the baby's eyes. In some babies given silver nitrate drops, the eyelids get puffy and there is a small amount of discharge. These reactions disappear in a few days. Delaying the treatment until an hour after birth will allow your baby to look at you with clear vision in the beginning.
Vitamin K treatment	Vitamin K is injected into the baby's thigh muscle approximately one hour after birth. (Oral forms of the vitamin are available, but many doctors consider them less effective than the injection.)	Vitamin K helps clot blood and protects against hemorrhaging. This vitamin is not present at birth, although it is produced in the baby's intestines as the baby begins to feed and reaches normal levels at about one week of age.	Treatment of all newborns is required by law in many states and provinces. Where it isn't required, some parents request that this painful injection not be given unless there is an indication of need.

Test for hypoglycemia (low blood sugar)	To determine the baby's blood glucose (sugar) level, blood is taken from the newborn's heel by pricking the heel with a microlancet.	Glucose, a major source of energy, is required for normal brain functioning. Low glucose levels can cause breathing difficulty, tremors, convulsions, and (in rare instances) death. Newborns who are considered at risk of hypoglycemia include those who are premature or post-mature, who are much larger than average or small for their gestational age, who have gotten chilled, who have nervous system disorders, or whose mothers have diabetes or received large amounts of sugarwater intravenously during labor.	Less pricking and squeezing may be needed if the baby's heel is heated before the test with a warm compress. Holding the baby during the test may also make it less stressful for both baby and parent. Treatment for hypoglycemia includes frequent feedings of milk, by breast or bottle, or giving glucose water by bottle, or both. If the baby cannot take food by mouth or the blood sugar level is very low, the baby may be given sugarwater intravenously.
Hepatitis B vaccination	Two injections are given to the newborn; one contains hepatitis B immune globulin (HBIG) and the other hepatitis B vaccine.	Hepatitis B is a serious disease that affects the liver. If a pregnant woman is infected, she can pass this virus to her baby during birth or afterward. If given shortly after birth, the vaccination can protect the baby from this illness. Additional doses are given at one month and six months of age.	The U.S. Centers for Disease Control have recommended hepatitis B vaccination of all newborns. This recommendation, however, has not been put into practice in all institutions. The American College of Obstetricians and Gynecologists recommends screening all pregnant women for hepatitis B, treating and counseling infected women during pregnancy, and identifying babies who will require vaccination at birth.

can go into the hospital nursery. The exams provide a wonderful opportunity to ask questions and learn about your baby.

Newborn Care—at Your Bedside or in the Nursery. Many hospitals now let each woman decide where her baby will be throughout her stay. If you keep your baby with you at all times, he or she will nurse more, bring your milk in sooner, lose less weight, and begin to develop a predictable sleep-wake pattern earlier than a baby who receives care from several people.

Some women ask that their babies be kept in the nursery at night but brought to them whenever the babies awaken hungry. Other women choose to have their babies spend time in the nursery when they themselves need naps during the day. A woman who has had a cesarean birth or a long, difficult labor may find having the baby in the nursery for several hours during each of the first days is critical to her recovery.

The needs of each mother and each baby are unique. Ask the staff at your hospital to help you arrange a care plan that suits your needs and wishes.

Blood Tests for Rare Diseases. A few babies who seem healthy at birth have hidden or rare diseases. If these diseases are found and treated early, serious health problems may be prevented. Most states and provinces require that tests for some of these rare diseases be done on all newborns before their discharge from a hospital or birth center. If your baby is born at home or discharged from the hospital within the first twenty-four hours, you may have to bring your baby to the doctor's office or arrange to have the tests done in your home before the baby reaches two weeks of age. Your baby's caregiver can tell you which tests are required in your state or province.

All of the tests are done by examining a few drops of blood taken from the baby's heel (see page 49). You will be notified of the results only if the baby tests positive for any of the diseases.

Jaundice. Jaundice is a yellowing of the skin and whites of the eyes. In itself, jaundice is not an illness. Jaundice indicates a buildup in the blood of bilirubin, which is produced when red

BLOOD TESTS FOR RARE DISEASES

Disorder	What Is It?	How Often Does It Occur?	What Is the Treatment?
Phenylketonuria (PKU)	An inherited disorder in which the baby lacks an enzyme needed to convert the amino acid phenylalanine into another amino acid, tyrosine. The buildup of phenylalanine in the bloodstream, if untreated, can lead to mental retardation.	1 baby in 15,000	A diet low in phenylalanine can prevent retardation; this diet may be needed through adolescence. At least partial breastfeeding may be possible, since breast milk is low in phenylalanine, but monitoring of phenylalanine levels is essential.* A specially modified formula is available for bottle feeding.
Galactosemia	An inherited disorder in which the baby lacks an enzyme needed to change galactose to glucose. The buildup of galactose in the body, if untreated, can lead to liver damage, cataracts, mental retardation, and death.	1 baby in 60,000	Treatment involves eliminating all milk, including breast milk, and lactose-containing foods from the diet. Affected infants are usually fed soy-based formula.
Hypothyroidism	This disorder has many causes. The most common is a defect in the development of the thyroid gland. If not treated, the disorder can cause mental retardation and stunt physical growth.	1 baby in 5,000	The treatment involves lifelong thyroid replacement therapy.
Hemoglobinopathy	An inherited disorder caused by changes in red blood cells. The disorder has several types, the most common of which is sickle-cell disease. This disease can affect all body systems and, if untreated, can cause anemia, pain, and death.	1 baby in 500 of African descent; the disorder is much less common and less severe in other populations	Sickle-cell disease is a lifelong condition that requires continuous treatment in various forms and prompt medical attention during any infection.

*Ruth A. Lawrence, *Breastfeeding: A Guide for the Medical Profession* (St. Louis: C. V. Mosby, 1985), 333–34.

blood cells are broken down, a normal process. A baby needs fewer red blood cells after birth than while in the womb, so a large quantity of red blood cells break down after birth. The human liver normally changes bilirubin so that it is easily excreted from the body. Newborns, however, have less efficient livers than older persons, so it is harder for them to clear bilirubin from their bodies. This can result in jaundice. Very high levels of bilirubin may be of concern because the newborn's neurological development may be affected.

The mildest form of jaundice is called *physiologic jaundice*. About 50 percent of full-term babies and as many as 80 percent of premature babies develop this. Physiologic jaundice appears after the first twenty-four hours; bilirubin levels are usually highest on the third day after birth. Then levels begin to drop, as bilirubin is excreted in feces. The jaundice disappears on its own by the end of the second week.

Newborns can also develop jaundice as the result of bruising during the birth process, use of certain drugs (the most common of which is Pitocin) in labor, and blood incompatibility with the mother.

A rare form of jaundice is called *breast-milk jaundice*. Occurring in fewer than 1 percent of breastfeeding infants, it is diagnosed by ruling out all other possible causes of jaundice. Breast-milk jaundice may not appear until the third to tenth day after birth, and bilirubin levels may not peak until the third week. The cause of breast milk jaundice is not definitely known.

If you notice that your baby is becoming jaundiced, notify the baby's caregiver. You will also want to call if the jaundice seems to be getting worse instead of better. In some cases, a doctor may order a blood test to determine the level of bilirubin in the baby's blood.

Whether and how a case of jaundice is treated depends on its cause and severity, the baby's maturity, and the caregiver's usual practice. Often the only treatment needed for physiologic jaundice is frequent feeding. Frequent feeding helps reduce jaundice by promoting bowel movements—especially if the food is colostrum, which has a laxative effect.

Some babies with jaundice are treated with phototherapy—by having the baby sleep undressed under special fluorescent lights.

In many areas, phototherapy can be done in the home, so the baby need not stay in the hospital.

If blood incompatibility is the cause of jaundice, and the case is severe, the baby may undergo an exchange transfusion of blood. This treatment, however, is used only very rarely.

In cases of breast-milk jaundice, treatment depends on bilirubin levels. The mother is sometimes advised to stop breastfeeding for a day or two (during which time she should express milk to maintain her supply). If this is recommended, ask about the risks and benefits of interrupting breastfeeding, and your alternatives. It is not necessary to quit breastfeeding permanently.

Circumcision. Circumcision is the cutting away of the *foreskin*, which covers the head of the penis, or the *glans*. Circumcision is done as part of a religious ritual and, in the United States, as a nonreligious custom. Doctors consider circumcision an elective procedure, that is, one that the parents may choose to have done, but that is not medically necessary.

The method used to perform circumcision depends on who does the procedure. If you are considering circumcision, ask your baby's caregiver how it is to be done and what the risks and benefits are. You will also want to be involved in the decision about who does the procedure. Circumcision may be done by an obstetrician, a pediatrician, or a family practitioner. In the Jewish tradition, circumcision is done on the eighth day after birth by a *mohel*, a person trained to perform this procedure but not to practice medicine.

In the hospital, circumcision is usually done before the mother and baby are discharged but after the first twenty-four hours, so the baby has a little time to adjust to life outside the womb first. The surgery takes about ten minutes. Healing takes a week to ten days. Possible complications include excessive bleeding, infection, and scarring.

Circumcision is painful. Many doctors now use local anesthesia during the procedure to reduce babies' pain and stress responses. On rare occasions, however, the anethesia causes bruising, bleeding, and tissue damage.

Care of the Circumcised Penis. After the circumcision the penis will be covered with gauze coated with petroleum jelly so that it is easy to remove. Once the dressing is removed, apply petroleum jelly after each diaper change so the irritated penis doesn't stick to the diaper.

Change diapers promptly to prevent urine and feces from irritating or infecting the wound. To wash the baby's bottom, use warm water without soap. The penis will look red and sore at first, and you may notice a tiny amount of bleeding. By the second day a yellowish substance will appear around the glans; this is a normal part of the healing process. **Warning signs** that you should immediately report to the baby's caregiver include bleeding, crusted yellow sores filled with cloudy fluid, swelling, and redness that persists beyond the first few days.

Care of the Uncircumcised Penis. Care of the uncircumcised penis is simple: you wash the glans and foreskin as a single unit. The foreskin cannot—and should not—be pulled back from the head of a newborn's penis. In 90 percent of boys, the foreskin becomes retractable by the age of three. Attempting to retract the foreskin before it has loosened on its own can result in scarring and constriction of the glans. When the foreskin becomes retractable, you or your son can cleanse the penis by pulling back the foreskin and washing underneath.

YOUR BABY'S BIRTH CERTIFICATE

In the United States, every birth is recorded with the department of health for the state in which the baby is born. Your baby's birth certificate will remain permanently on file in the state in which you gave birth. Before leaving the hospital or birth center, ask how to obtain a copy of the baby's birth certificate. In some states, city or county agencies issue birth certificates. In others only the state health department can issue them. You may need your baby's birth certificate as proof of citizenship, to have a passport issued for your child, and to register your child in school. Most agencies charge a fee to issue a birth certificate.

When you obtain your certificate, do check it for accuracy. If you should find any errors, immediately notify the agency that issued it.

Health Care Beyond the First Days

If you did not select a caregiver for your baby before the birth, this is one of the first things you will want to do afterward. Once you have chosen a caregiver, that person will be available to you by phone should you have questions about your baby's well-being before the first checkup.

If your baby's health care will be covered by an insurance plan, review your policy. It will tell you which caregivers and services are covered, at what rates, and when coverage begins for your baby.

Learning about Your Health Care Options. Depending on where you live, you may have a number of choices in health care for your baby. Here are some options you may have in your community:

- *Family practitioners*: A family practitioner is a medical doctor who cares for people of all age groups—from infants to the elderly. This is a good choice if you would like to have one doctor serve the whole family. Family practitioners may work alone or in a group practice.
- *Pediatricians*: Pediatricians are medical doctors who specialize in the care of children, from birth through the teen years. Pediatricians may work alone or in a group practice.
- *Pediatric nurse practitioners (PNPs)*: PNPs are registered nurses who have received additional schooling and training that enables them to specialize in well-child care. They usually work in partnership with pediatricians or family practitioners, with whom they consult when children are ill. PNPs spend a large part of well-baby visits teaching parents about babies and their care.
- *Public health clinics*: Available in many communities, public health clinics may provide care for both well and sick children or may offer only well-child checkups or immunizations. Some public health clinics offer other important services, such as nutrition education and social services. In the United States, some provide vouchers for WIC (see page 18). The services may be free, or the clinic may have a sliding fee scale.

  Your public health agency may also be able to send a *visiting nurse* to your home. A visiting nurse can help you learn about taking care of the baby, and help you find other community services that may make life with the new baby easier. Most new parents find these visits very reassuring. If you would like to have a visiting nurse come to your home after childbirth, ask your midwife or doctor to help you arrange the visit.

Good sources of information about health care for children may include friends, family members, your doctor or midwife, and local hospitals. For information about public health services, call your city, county, or state or provincial health department.

Selecting the Caregiver Best for You. What do you look for when selecting a caregiver or clinic? Here are some questions other parents have considered in deciding who will provide care for their children:

- Do you feel comfortable with the caregiver? With the office or clinic environment?
- Does the caregiver invite your participation in decision making about the care your baby will receive?
- Do you feel this person will support parenting decisions you may have already made, such as how you will feed your baby?
- With which hospitals does the caregiver work?
- When will the caregiver see you and your baby after the birth?
- Is the office conveniently situated?
- What are the office hours? Is the office open evenings or weekends?
- How long, on average, do clients have to wait in the waiting room?
- Are sick and well children provided with separate waiting areas?
- How many practitioners work in the office? Can parents select one caregiver who will usually see their baby?
- What is the cost of a well-baby visit? A visit with a sick child?
- Will the office bill your insurance company directly?
- How far in advance must you schedule routine checkups?
- If you call with questions about your baby, how soon does the caregiver return phone calls? If your baby is ill in the middle of the night or when the office is closed, what procedures must you follow to obtain advice or treatment?

If you phone the office of each caregiver you are considering, a receptionist or nurse will be able to provide answers to many of your questions. The rest can be answered in a visit with the caregiver; most are happy to meet with parents who are considering using them. A fee may or may not be charged for this consultation.

If, after taking your baby to a caregiver, you feel dissatisfied with the choice you have made, you *can* change to a different one. After all, you'll probably be seeing the caregiver you settle on for several years, or longer. It is worth the effort to make sure you've chosen someone whose service and personal style meet your needs and expectations.

Well-Baby Care and Immunizations. The first well-baby checkup is usually scheduled for two weeks after the birth. At this visit your baby's caregiver will give you a schedule for future well-baby checkups. These checkups provide measures of your baby's health and development, and opportunities for early response to any health problems.

Part of well-child care is immunization against potentially serious illnesses. Before having your baby immunized, you should make sure your baby's caregiver knows if—

- Your baby is, or has recently been, sick.
- Your baby has had convulsions or other health problems affecting the nervous system.
- Your baby has an allergy to eggs (which are used to manufacture the MMR vaccine).
- Your baby has had a reaction to a previous immunization.
- Another child in your family has had a reaction to an immunization.
- Your baby has a weakened immune system, or is receiving any medication that affects the immune system.

Your caregiver will probably give you an informational brochure about each immunization your child is to receive. Such brochures provide information on the disease or diseases that the immunization can prevent, known side effects of the immunization, and how to care for your baby afterward. You may be asked to sign a form

GENERAL U.S. IMMUNIZATION SCHEDULE

Baby's age	Vaccine
2 months	• DPT (diphtheria, pertussis, tetanus) • Polio • HBCV (Haemophilus B Conjugate Vaccine, which protects against bacterial infections caused by *Haemophilus influenzae B*)
4 months	• DPT • HBCV • Polio
6 months	• DPT • HBCV
15 months	• MMR (measles, mumps, rubella) • HBCV
15 to 18 months	• DPT • Polio
4 to 6 years	• DPT • Polio
11 to 12 years	• MMR
14 to 16 years	• DT (diphtheria, tetanus)

Source: Steven P. Shelov *et al.*, eds., *Caring for Your Baby and Young Child: Birth to Age Five* (New YorK: Bantam, 1991), 3.

that states you have received this information and agree to having the immunization done.

Signs of Illness in a Newborn. Many parents doubt whether they will recognize if the baby is sick. When you have no experience with babies, being told that a sick baby behaves differently from a well baby is of little comfort. If everything about your baby seems unfamiliar, it is hard to have confidence that you can and will recognize changes that indicate your baby is ill. Besides, healthy babies can cry for a couple of hours each day. Crying does not tell you as much in the first weeks as it will when your baby is older. So how will you know if your baby is sick? Asking yourself these questions may help:

- *Is there a change in the baby's behavior?* Is the baby crying more than usual? Has the tone of the cry changed? Is the crying at a different time of day than usual? Is the baby more irritable than usual?

   Is the baby sleeping more or less than usual? Does the baby seem lethargic or listless?
- *Has the baby's appetite or digestion changed?* Is the baby eating less than usual?

   Has the baby vomited more than once? If the baby is vomiting, is the vomiting forceful? (This is called *projectile* vomiting.)

   Are there signs of constipation? That is, are the stools hard or more solid than usual?

   Are there signs of diarrhea? That is, are the stools watery, or more runny than usual? Are they more frequent than usual? (See page 68.)

   Is the baby urinating less frequently than usual? Has the color of the urine changed?
- *Has there been a change in the baby's breathing?* Does the baby seem to have trouble breathing? Does the baby sound congested? Does the baby have a runny or stuffy nose? Is the baby coughing? (See pages 66–67.)
- *How does the baby look?* Is the baby's skin pale or flushed? Is there a rash anywhere on the baby's body? Do the baby's eyes look glassy or dull? Is there any discharge from the eyes?
- *Does the baby have a fever?* (See pages 58–59.)

Any of these changes could indicate illness. If you notice any of them, or other worrisome changes in your baby, call your baby's caregiver. When you call the office, be prepared to describe:

- The signs of illness about which you are concerned.
- How long the signs have been present.
- What you need: to have the caregiver return your call; to speak to the caregiver immediately, if you feel this is an emergency; or to arrange for the baby to be seen as soon as possible.

How to Take Your Baby's Temperature. There are two ways to take a baby's temperature—under the arm or in the rectum. (Most children won't keep a thermometer in their mouths until they are

---

If your baby has any of the following, immediately call 911 or take the baby to the nearest emergency room.

• Any serious accident or injury to any part of the body
• Unconsciousness
• Convulsions
• Bleeding that cannot be stopped
• Black stools after the first few days, or any signs of blood in the stool
• Sunken eyes
• Sunken or bulging fontanels (the soft spots on the baby's head)
• Bluish or greyish skin

---

about five years old.) Before taking the temperature either way, wash the thermometer with soap and cold water. Then check the thermometer's current reading. If the reading is above 96 degrees Fahrenheit, firmly hold the thermometer between your thumb and forefinger, on the end opposite the bulb. Shake the thermometer, by snapping your wrist, until the mercury reading is below 96.

Axillary temperature. The underarm, or *axillary*, method is the easiest and the least stressful for both parent and baby. You can use either an oral or a rectal thermometer. Definitely take an axillary rather than a rectal temperature if you have only an oral thermometer or if the baby has diarrhea.

To take an axillary temperature, remove the baby's clothing from the waist up. Place the bulb end of the thermometer in the armpit, and hold the arm snugly against the baby's side (see illustration). Keep the thermometer in place at least four minutes (sometimes it takes more than five minutes) while you sing or talk to the baby. A normal axillary temperature is 97.6 degrees Fahrenheit.

Rectal temperature. To take a *rectal* temperature, be sure to use a rectal, not an oral, thermometer. Lubricate the bulb end of the thermometer with petroleum jelly, applied with a cotton ball. Lay the baby, bare-bottomed and tummy down, on your lap. As you talk soothingly to the baby, spread the buttocks with one hand until you can see the anus, which opens into the rectum. With the other hand, gently slip the lubricated end of the thermometer about 1 inch into the rectum (see illustration). Keep the thermometer in place for one to three minutes, while you sing or talk to the baby. A normal rectal temperature is 99.6 degrees Fahrenheit.

After taking the baby's temperature, wash the thermometer with cold water and soap, then wipe it with an alcohol-soaked cotton ball. Let it dry. Store the thermometer in its protective case away from any heat.

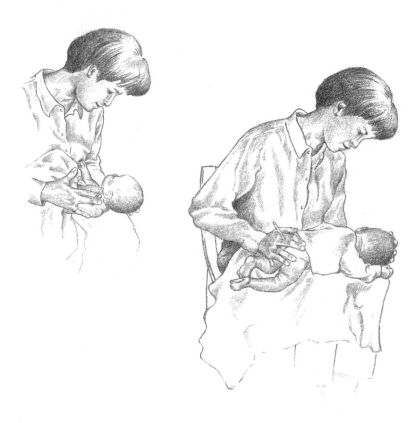

Taking an axillary temperature (left) and a rectal temperature (right).

More and more new parents are taking classes in infant and child cardiopulmonary resuscitation (CPR). Such a course can teach you what to do in the event your baby chokes on an object or stops breathing. CPR is easy to learn, and it saves lives. If you are interested in taking a class, contact your local Red Cross, Y, or hospital. Your baby's caregiver can probably refer you to programs in your area.

Sudden Infant Death Syndrome (SIDS): Sometimes called crib death, SIDS is the sudden, unexpected, and unexplainable death of an infant in the first year after birth. Among infants over one month old, SIDS is the most frequent cause of death. Ninety percent of SIDS deaths occur in babies less than six months old.

SIDS is naturally a source of concern for expectant and new parents, and many ask what causes SIDS and how it can be prevented. Unfortunately, there are no clear answers to either of these questions. Although researchers are exploring possible causes, the syndrome is still considered unpredictable and unpreventable. We know that SIDS is not hereditary; it is not caused by external suffocation or by vomiting or choking.

Recently, research has suggested that a newborn's position during sleep may be related to SIDS. Because of these studies, the American Academy of Pediatrics recommended in 1992 that babies be placed on their sides or backs for sleep rather than on their stomachs. Much controversy exists about this recommendation. You may wish to consult your baby's caregiver for the latest information on this and other aspects of SIDS.[1]

Safe Travel with Your Baby. Every U.S. state now requires the use of car safety seats for children under four years of age. All car seats manufactured from 1981 on must meet federal safety standards. Using a federally approved car seat has been shown to reduce greatly the chances of death or injury to children involved in car accidents.

You can find car seats in discount and children's stores. Hospitals and health departments often have car seat rental programs or can direct you to such programs in your community. If you're considering using a secondhand car seat, check its label to be sure it meets federal standards.

Infant car seats, which always face the rear of the car, are safe for children up to twenty pounds. Infant-toddler car seats can be set up one way for a baby up to twenty pounds, then adjusted for use until the child is forty pounds or four years old. A car seat may be ineffective if used incorrectly, so do read and follow the directions that come with yours.

Your newborn will be more comfortable in the car seat if you place a foam cushion or rolled towel around the baby's head to support it. In hot weather, cover the car seat with a towel before placing your baby in it.

Your Newborn's Characteristics

When parents first greet their babies, they often speak of counting fingers and toes. In the next few hours, they usually look much closer at their newborns. Most parents quickly note a likeness between their babies and particular family members. "He looks like Aunt Anne," they say, or "She has Grandma's eyes."

Sheila Kitzinger, a British anthropologist and childbirth educator, talks about the baby "unfolding" in the first days after birth.[2] This lovely image captures the change in appearance that babies undergo in the first hours and days.

The Baby's Head. The baby's head is large in proportion to the rest of the body; it makes up about 25 percent of the total body length. The head is often *molded*, which usually means it is more egg-shaped than rounded. Molding happens when the baby moves through the pelvis, cervix, and vagina during labor. (A baby born face up rather than face down at birth may have a more dome-shaped than egg-shaped head.) The head becomes more rounded in the first couple of days after birth. Babies born by cesarean show very little molding unless the surgery was done after the mother was in labor for a time.

The bones on your baby's head will not be firmly set until your baby is about eighteen months old. This allows the brain to continue its growth. You will notice that your baby's head has two soft spots, called *fontanels*. One, shaped like a diamond, is just above the forehead. This will close between eighteen and twenty-four months of age. The other, shaped like a triangle, is toward the back of the head. It will close by about six months of age. Don't be afraid to touch or wash these areas; your baby's brain is well protected by thick tissues.

The baby's scalp may look wrinkled, especially at the moment of birth. The baby might have a swelling on the scalp, called a *caput*, caused by a buildup of fluid from pressure on that area during labor. The bump will disappear within a week or so of birth.

Several hours after birth a *cephalhematoma* might appear on one or the other side of the head. A collection of blood between the skull bone and the membrane covering it, a cephalhematoma is caused by pressure during birth. The swelling is largest on the second or third day after birth, but then the bleeding stops. There is no bleeding into the brain, and no treatment is required. The cephalhematoma will disappear in three to six weeks.

It is not unusual for a newborn to have small bruise marks on the head or face after birth. These bruises heal in a matter of days.

The Baby's Hair. Some newborns have very little hair; others have quite a lot. Over the next few months the first hair will be replaced and may change colors.

You may notice fine hair over large parts of the baby's body. This *lanugo* disappears within a week or so of birth.

Vernix. At birth your baby may be covered with a thick, white, creamy substance. This substance, called *vernix*, is produced by skin cells to form a protective coating over much of your baby's body during pregnancy. Some babies have more vernix at birth than others.

The Baby's Skin. A newborn's skin is as soft as velvet. For a few hours after birth, a baby may appear deep red in color. Then the skin lightens to a pinkish tone. Infants whose parents have dark skin are somewhat lighter in color than their parents at birth. The skin color darkens gradually over time.

You may note a blotchy discoloration of the skin on your baby's trunk or legs. This mottling occurs when the newborn is chilled and disappears when the baby is warmed.

The hands and feet of all newborns also become slightly bluish off and on for the first seven to ten days. This is most obvious when the baby is chilled, but you may notice it even when the baby is comfortably warm, especially if he or she is asleep. When the baby moves, the extremities return to their normal color. All of these variations in color are due primarily to the infant's immature circulatory system.

On your baby's cheeks, forehead, and nose, you may notice *milia*. These tiny, pearly white spots are undeveloped or blocked sweat glands. Milia often appear on the second day and usually disappear by the second week after birth. They do not require any treatment.

A few days after birth, the baby's skin may become dry and flaky, especially around the hands and the feet. Sometimes this flakiness is seen at birth if the baby is several days overdue. It is not necessary to use lotion or any other moisturizer on this dry skin. The peeling may continue for two to four weeks.

A *newborn rash* can appear suddenly on any part of the baby's body in the first weeks. The most common sort of newborn rash has red spots with yellowish centers. This rash may appear on the back, abdomen, shoulders, and buttocks. It does not need treatment, and it usually disappears entirely in a day or so.

Colorings and birthmarks. Several kinds of colorings and markings are common on newborns. Pale pink spots, called angel kisses, frequently appear on eyelids and between the eyebrows. Similar spots on the back of the head and neck are called stork bites. Both disappear almost completely by the baby's first birthday.

Red to purple "port-wine stains," the most common sort of birthmark, may be found on almost any part of the body. These may not disappear completely, but they usually fade so much that they are only noticeable when the baby is upset.

"Strawberry marks," the second most common type of birthmark, look like the surface of a ripe strawberry. Raised and bright red, they may be present at birth or appear any time in the first six weeks. Sometimes strawberry marks get bigger in the first few months after birth, but this growth stops completely by the end of the first year. After that the marks begin to shrink. Strawberry marks eventually disappear, usually by the age of ten.

Some babies have bluish-black areas on the back, buttocks, belly, arms, or legs. Usually, these "Mongolian spots" are present at birth and gone by age one. Occasionally, however, they do not appear until later, and they may persist into adulthood. They are common in infants of Asian, Latin American, and African descent.

None of these skin colorings or markings indicate anything is wrong with a baby; none require treatment. Many parents, however, feel sad when they see such marks. If your baby has any of them, you may want to discuss them with your baby's caregiver. He or she can reassure you that both the colorings and your feelings about them are normal.

The Baby's Eyes. Newborns' eyes are beautifully colored. Caucasian babies' eyes are usually dark to slate blue. Asian and African-American babies usually have dark brown eyes at birth. By the time your baby is six months old, you'll see your baby's permanent eye color, though the depth of color may not be obvious until your baby is a year old. Your baby's eyes will change in other ways, too. In the first days after birth, one or both of the baby's eyelids may be puffy—just as the whole face and body may be. There may be tiny patches of red on the whites of the eyes; these disappear in a few days. And, since babies' eye movements aren't fully coordinated at first, sometimes the eyes will look crossed. All these characteristics are temporary.

When your newborn cries, you probably won't see tears. Infants usually don't produce tears when crying until they are about one month old.

Because newborns' tear ducts are tiny, they sometimes get plugged. This happens in one in 100 babies. A baby with a plugged tear duct may accumulate yellowish-white mucus in the inner corner of the eye, and the eyelids may be stuck together with crusty mucus when the baby awakens. He or she may have a teary-eyed look, even when happy, because the glands over the eyes that produce the tear overflow. You can cleanse the eye by gently wiping it with a sterile cotton ball moistened with water that has been boiled and cooled. You may be able to open the duct by gently massaging it; ask your baby's caregiver how to do this.

A plugged duct is different from an eye infection. Signs of infection are thick, dark yellow mucus and reddening of the whites of the eyes. These signs should be promptly reported to the baby's caregiver.

The Baby's Mouth. Most babies develop sucking blisters on the upper lip after the first few feedings. These do not require any treatment.

If you look into your baby's mouth, you may notice several things. There are thick pads on the insides of the cheeks; these facilitate breastfeeding. The baby's tongue is large in proportion to the mouth, and it sticks out a bit when the baby's mouth is open. This is because the infant's tongue is especially designed for sucking rather than for eating solid foods. Your baby may also have yellowish white spots along the gum margins and at the point where the hard and soft palates meet. These spots, which doctors call *Epstein's pearls*, are normal. They disappear in the first month after birth.

White patches in the mouth or throat that bleed if touched are *not* normal. They may be *thrush*, a common yeast infection that a baby can get during passage through the vagina. Notify your baby's caregiver if you notice such patches.

The Baby's Fingernails. Although at birth your baby's fingernails will probably extend beyond the ends of the finger tips, you shouldn't cut the nails for at least the first week, because the nail tips are at first still connected to the nail beds. Cutting them too early could cause a tiny amount of bleeding—which would be upsetting for both you and the baby. When you are ready to cut the nails, you may find it easier to do when the baby is sound asleep.

Because their nails are long, babies often scratch themselves. These scratches, which heal quickly, are usually more worrisome for the parents than the baby. Many newborn gowns and T-shirts have cloth covers for the hands; you can use these until you cut the nails, if you wish. Some babies, however, find comfort in putting their fingers into their mouths. Cloth covers on the hands make this impossible. If your baby puts his or her fingers in the mouth for comfort, be grateful! This self-comforting skill can make life easier for you and your baby.

The Baby's Breasts and Sex Organs. At birth, the breasts of both boys and girls are commonly somewhat swollen. This swelling disappears in two to three weeks. Sometimes tiny amounts of fluid come from the baby's breasts. It is important not to massage the baby's breasts or try to squeeze out this fluid because doing so could cause an infection.

Newborn girls have swollen and reddened labia (the lips around the vaginal opening). You may also notice a tiny discharge of blood or a clear or whitish discharge from the baby's vagina. Both the swelling and the discharge, normal effects of exposure to the mother's hormones, disappear in a matter of days.

Maternal hormones may also make a newborn boy's scrotum (the sac that holds the testicles) swollen and reddish for a day or so after birth.

The testicles develop in the abdomen during pregnancy and usually descend into the scrotum just before birth. Occasionally, though, one or both testicles have not descended by the time the baby is born. In time, testicles usually descend. But should you notice that one or both testicles are not in the scrotum, discuss this with your baby's caregiver. He or she will check for their presence at each well-baby visit.

The Baby's Breathing. A newborn breathes at a rate of twenty to forty breaths per minute. The breathing rate and depth vary depending on the baby's activity or sleep state. Babies breathe with their bellies, so it is normal to see abdominal movement when you watch your baby breathe. Babies occasionally hold their breath for a few seconds. Frequent breath holding, or any breath holding for longer than ten seconds, should be reported to the baby's caregiver.

Babies make many different kinds of noises when they breath. Mucus in the nose or throat can result in loud breathing sounds. You might ask your nurse or midwife to teach you how to use a bulb syringe to remove mucus from the nose and mouth. Use the bulb syringe sparingly—and only if the mucus is bothering the baby more than being suctioned would.

Signs of illness are fast breathing (more than sixty breaths per minute), sucking in (*refraction*) of the muscles between the ribs with each breath, frequent flaring of the nostrils or grunting, and a bluish skin color. Any of these signs should be reported to the baby's caregiver.

The Baby's Body Temperature. The average body temperature among healthy newborns is 98.6 degrees Fahrenheit. Your baby's own average temperature may be slightly different than this—say, 98 or 99 degrees.

From the moment of birth, newborns produce body heat like older people. But young babies are not as good as older persons at conserving heat; they lose it about as fast as they produce it. If chilled, the baby must burn extra calories to keep warm. Calories burned to keep warm cannot be used for normal growth and development.

Because of this it is important to keep your baby warm. The amount of clothing he or she needs, of course, depends on your climate, whether the baby is indoors or out, and, when indoors, how warm your house is. As a rule of thumb, your newborn needs one more layer of clothing or covering than you need. When you bathe the baby, make sure the room is free of drafts and comfortably warm. In cooler weather, cover your baby with an extra blanket when he or she is sleeping.

Your baby will be much better at conserving heat by the time he or she grows to twelve pounds or reaches three months of age. Then you can dress the baby with the same amount of clothing you need to feel comfortable.

Overheating is a danger for babies, too. Sometimes babies get heat rash, or "prickly heat"—tiny red bumps in the skin folds, especially on the neck, shoulders, bottom, and cheeks. If you see this rash, keep the baby's skin cool and dry. Call the baby's caregiver if blisters appear on the red bumps. A baby who gets overheated can experience not only a rash but heatstroke—a serious illness that can cause death. Signs of heatstroke are hot skin, fever, diarrhea, agitation or lethargy, and convulsions or loss of consciousness. Immediate medical care is needed.

To avoid overheating, be careful not to overdress your baby. In hot weather, dress the baby in light, loose-fitting, natural-fiber clothes. Never leave your baby unattended in direct sunlight or in a parked car, even with the windows down. In cool weather, when you bring the baby in from outdoors, be sure to remove the snow suit or bunting. Since babies often fall asleep on outings, it is tempting to leave on the winter clothing until the baby awakens. The baby can, however, get overheated. Finally, a baby with a fever should not be bundled in blankets.

A baby's initial response to being too cool or too warm is to fuss. You will want to consider this when you go through the mental checklist all parents consult when their babies are restless or crying.

The Baby's Bowel Movements and Urine. Babies usually have their first bowel movements within twenty-four hours of birth. The first several stools consist of *meconium*—a greenish-black, sticky, semisolid substance that is in the baby's intestines before birth.

As the meconium is expelled, the baby's stools change. Formula-fed babies have light brown, seedy-looking stools. Breastfed babies' stools become mustard yellow and semiliquid. Their runny character often makes parents worry that their babies have diarrhea. But diarrhea looks quite different—it often contains mucus and it is watery, not just runny. It usually has a bad odor, unlike the strong sweet smell of the stools breastfed babies usually have.

Occasionally, parents notice a trace of blood in a baby's stool in the first day or two after birth. This is usually maternal blood that the baby swallowed during the birth; it does not harm the baby. But the baby's caregiver should be notified so an exam can be done to ensure the baby is well.

Many babies strain, grunt, and become red in the face when having a bowel movement. This is not due to constipation.

Each baby develops his or her own pattern of bowel movements. In the first weeks, a breastfed baby may have a stool four or five times a day; formula-fed babies may have somewhat fewer stools. After four to five weeks, breastfed babies often have less frequent bowel movements; some even go a few days between stools. This is because more mature babies are better at digesting all the nutrients in breast milk. In the first month after birth, however, infrequent bowel movements are a sign to contact the baby's caregiver.

Newborns usually urinate twelve times or more in a twenty-four-hour period. You should expect at least eight wet diapers a day by the time the baby is five days old. The great absorbency of disposable diapers can make it hard for parents to know if the baby has urinated. But even if a diaper doesn't feel wet, it will feel heavier than a dry diaper if the baby has urinated. Wet diapers, as well as bowel movements, are important indications that a baby is getting enough milk.

You will really know you have entered a new stage in your life when you find that the frequency, color, and quantity of your baby's wastes have become a frequent subject of conversation. This is all part of the art of "paying attention," whether or not the most fun part. Welcome to the world of parenting!

Your Newborn's Sensory Skills

Of all of the things that are marvelous about a baby, the baby's ability to both respond to people and to initiate interaction is perhaps the most amazing. In the first four to six weeks after birth, this ability is easy to miss if you don't know what to watch for—or if you don't quite believe what you see.

Experienced parents of healthy, happy children will tell you that most of parenting is a matter of paying attention—of following as much as leading. Pregnancy begins to teach parents this skill. As a woman's pregnancy progresses, she often finds herself focused inward, attending to her baby's rhythms and activity. The expectant mate usually becomes a great observer of the pregnant woman, developing deeper awareness of her body language, her feelings, and her needs. This alertness in expectant parents serves them well when they become mothers and fathers. It is what eventually leads children to believe that their parents have "eyes in the back of the head," supernatural hearing, and an uncanny ability to detect trouble when "things are too quiet." These skills are simply evidence of the way in which parents pay attention—not only with their minds and their hearts, but with all of their senses.

Newborns also pay attention to the world with all of their senses. They are born with reflexes that make the world accessible to them. They can exert some control over how things affect them by becoming more or less alert, by crying, and by entering different sleep states. They can communicate using body movements and facial expressions.

This section is about the things that new babies can do. It includes suggestions for ways to enjoy your baby and to make your baby's world an interesting and safe place. When you pay attention, your baby can guide you into parenting. As your baby guides you into parenting, you can confidently guide your baby into the world.

The Baby's Vision. A newborn can most clearly see a face or an object about 8 inches away. (If you are holding your baby in your arms for a feeding, 8 to 12 inches is the distance from the crook of your arm to your eyes.) Gradually, the baby becomes able to focus on things farther away. By four to six months of age, a baby's vision is as good as an adult's.

Babies spend a lot of time looking into the distance, especially at contrasts in lighting. You may find yourself looking over your shoulder to see what the baby is studying.

Babies enjoy looking at faces. They seem to know what a human face is supposed to look like. So if you show a new baby a picture of a face with one eye in the middle, the baby will show less interest in it than in a picture of a face that has two eyes where they are supposed to be.

In the first weeks, the boundaries of the face may sometimes fascinate your baby more than the center of the face. This is because things that contrast attract the newborn's attention. Your hairline, as well as your eyes and your mouth, contrasts with your skin.

The marvelous thing about faces is that they are constantly changing. This is probably one of the reasons babies spend so much time looking at them. Babies are doing more than looking; they are learning while they watch. You can teach a baby only a few hours old to stick out his or her tongue. It is fun to watch a baby practice until he or she gets this skill just right. Babies will mimic opening the mouth wide, also. So, from birth, infants do what they see.

Newborns can be overstimulated by what they see. In the early weeks, you will want your baby's sleeping area to be visually soothing. Avoid the temptation to buy sheets with bright or bold patterns; white or soft pastels are best. (Even adults have been shown to be overstimulated by bedding that has too much color or contrast, making their sleep more difficult.) Keep the sleep area free of clutter. It will be at least a month, anyway, before your baby shows interest in stuffed animals, mirrors, toys, or mobiles. When your baby is two to three months old, you can place one or two baby-safe toys in the crib for the baby to study when awake and alert. Soon after, your baby will begin to have conversations with the face in the baby mirror or the toy animal with the smiling face.

As the baby develops interest in the world beyond your arms, you can place interesting pictures or other objects around the changing area. When you choose things for your baby's entertainment, look at them from the angle from which your baby will see them. A lot of things you may find in stores for babies are actually designed to attract an older person's attention; when viewed from the baby's angle, they are of little interest. By the way, your baby doesn't care if the interesting item you offer for viewing is a colorful kitchen towel or a Renoir painting, a picture from a magazine or from the National Gallery of Art. The important thing is to change items often. Since babies learn quickly, they show more interest in the unfamiliar than the familiar. You will want to provide your baby with different items to explore every week or so.

The Baby's Hearing. Your baby can hear clearly at birth. The baby has, in fact, heard the world around you during the last four months of pregnancy. Because of this, the sounds of other children in your home, pets, traffic around your house, and even planes overhead may all have become familiar to your baby before birth. Because normal household sounds are already familiar to the baby, he or she will usually be able to sleep right through them. Indeed, some sounds from prenatal life can actually calm the baby. Soothing music played in pregnancy can help a baby to sleep after birth. Audiotapes of placental sounds or of a heartbeat can also comfort a baby. You don't need a tape, of course, to comfort your baby with the sound of a heartbeat. Just place your baby against your chest.

Babies often slip into sleep when confronted with "white noise." Parents of fussy babies often use this knowledge to their advantage.

Many a parent has placed the cradle near a running dishwasher or clothes dryer as a way of quieting a baby who seems to be having a hard day.

Newborns are attracted to human voices as well as faces. The high-pitched, soft voice parents often use when talking to babies attracts their attention. A baby responds to a voice by turning toward its source, or, if the voice is too stimulating, by turning away. Both responses can guide new parents in interactions with the baby.

The Baby's Senses of Smell and Taste. Babies have a well-developed sense of smell. Newborns turn away from unpleasant odors and turn towards odors that are pleasant. They quickly learn to distinguish between their mothers' odors and those of others, and within days of birth can identify their mothers by smell alone.

Babies also have an acute sense of taste; they actually have more taste buds than adults do. They can tell the difference between sweet, salty, and sour, and they prefer sweet tastes. It is *not* a good idea, however, to sweeten formula or water to entice the baby to drink. Sugar can cause diarrhea, and honey should not be fed to a baby under one year of age. Honey can cause infant botulism, a form of food poisoning.

The Baby's Sense of Touch. Touch is the first of the unborn baby's senses to develop. A newborn feels the world with his or her whole body. Touch is so important to babies that they cannot thrive without it.

Most newborn babies love to be held but dislike being manipulated. This is probably why diapering and dressing a brand-new baby causes many new parents to break into a cold sweat. Fortunately for newborns, new parents work very hard at being gentle. You may be surprised at how fast you learn to handle the baby with confidence—and how fast the baby overcomes that initial hypersensitivity to all the new sensations involved in being cared for.

Because of the comfort of touch and closeness, many babies want to spend a good part of their day—and night—next to a parent. In the first month after birth, babies are not really aware of themselves as separate from you. *It is OK to keep your baby near you.* This will not spoil a newborn.

Keeping the baby close to you not only promotes growth and development, it also results in less crying. One research study found that babies who were held for at least three hours besides when they were crying or being fed cried much less than babies who were held only for feeding or when crying.[3] Using a cloth sling or baby pack can be an easy way to keep your baby near you. (It can also make it possible to do a few things other than just hold the baby. In the real world of real parenting, this is important in maintaining your sanity.)

Infant massage can be another way of responding to your baby's need for touch. Many parents massage their babies daily. Massage has been effectively used to calm fussy babies, reduce colic, and even promote the development of premature infants.[4] It also nurtures the growing bond between parent and baby. Pick a time of day to do massage when the baby is awake and content. Make sure the room is warm. If it soothes the baby, play soft music or sing or talk quietly to your baby. You can use oil, if you like, that you have in your kitchen, such as olive, safflower, or sunflower oil. Warm it in your hands before applying it.

Pay attention to your baby's cues about being massaged. If the baby remains calm, alert, and relaxed, you can be confident that the baby is enjoying the experience. A newborn may most enjoy massage of the legs and feet. When the baby gets a few weeks older, he or she will probably like being massaged on the abdomen, chest, arms, hands, face, and back. If the baby fusses or seems tense, this might not be the right time for the massage. Some babies, especially those who are very sensitive to tactile stimulation, may not tolerate massage at all until they are several weeks old. Let your baby be your guide.

Infant massage classes are offered in many communities. They can be a great place to meet other new parents.

Your Newborn's Reflexes and Motor Skills

A reflex is an automatic response of the nervous system that does not require thought. If you tap the tendon in your knee, for example, your leg moves without your thinking about it. You'll notice several reflexes in watching or handling your newborn. These reflexes form the basis for your newborn's motor behavior; learned behaviors are built on these reflexes. They give your baby an opportunity to interact with his or her environment from the moment of birth. You may want to ask a nurse or your baby's caregiver to demonstrate your newborn's reflexes for you.

The Rooting and Sucking Reflexes. When you gently stroke the baby's cheek or the corner of the mouth, the baby will turn towards the touch and open his or her mouth. This rooting reflex is the way the baby searches for food. The sucking reflex can be felt when putting a bottle or pacifier nipple or a clean finger into the baby's mouth—and, of course, when breastfeeding. Both the rooting and sucking reflexes are strongest when the baby is hungry. Hungry babies root against anything that touches their faces, including blankets, parents' arms, and their own hands. Bringing hands up against the side of the head or to the mouth, as uncoordinated as these movements may look, are a very clear sign of hunger.

Putting a baby to breast in the first hour after birth stimulates the sucking reflex. It also impresses on the baby the feel of the breast. Some newborns show a marked preference for the first object that satisfies their sucking need. For this reason many lactation consultants recommend that, if breastfeeding must be delayed, the baby be fed with a dropper. Using an artificial nipple can lead to "nipple confusion." This is one example of how a reflex action (sucking) leads to a learned behavior (sucking from a breast or artificial nipple). A nipple-confused baby *can* learn to suck from a breast, but may have a harder time doing so.

Many medications used for pain relief in labor—including both narcotics and regional anesthetics—weaken the sucking reflex in the newborn. This can lead to frustration for a breastfeeding mother. Don't get discouraged; give the baby time to learn, and don't hesitate to ask for assistance. You and your baby will be able to do it. Even unmedicated babies often take two or three days to learn to nurse effectively.

To manage the flow of milk, your baby sucks in bursts and pauses. As the baby gets good at this, he or she will use the pauses to invite interaction with you. When the baby pauses, you may speak to the baby. The more often you speak, the more frequently the baby pauses. Unless you are in a great hurry, you will find feeding time becomes a very social time, too. This social exchange between parent and baby is as important as the feeding, and worth all the time it takes.

In the first months, infants suck not just to satisfy hunger, but also as a way of calming themselves. You may notice that your baby even sucks during sleep. Some newborns are very good at bringing their hands to their mouths and sucking on their fingers, wrists, or entire hands.

Some infants with strong sucking needs prefer pacifiers to hands or fingers. If you are breastfeeding, wait until you've nursed your baby successfully for a few days before trying a pacifier. Then, if you want to give your baby a pacifier, select one in which the nipple does not separate from the mouth guard or handle. Make sure the mouth guard is at least 2 inches wide, is flat, and has air holes for breathing. The package label should indicate that the material from which the pacifier is made is nontoxic.

If your baby takes to the pacifier, wash it daily in mild soap, and rinse it well. If it drops onto the floor or an unclean surface, wash it before giving it back to the baby. Replace the pacifier as soon as it shows signs of deterioration, such as stickiness or tiny cracks. Never attach a pacifier to a string tied around the baby's neck; this could result in strangulation.

Some babies need to suck more than others, and different babies have different ways of satisfying their sucking needs. Parents are often surprised that what satisfied one of their babies does not work as well with another. One baby may suck on her hands and refuse a pacifier; another may suck on a pacifier, but not his hands. Some will enjoy both, and some will be satisfied by nothing but the breast. This is only one example of how unique each baby is.

The Grasp Reflex. When you place your finger in the palm of your baby's hand or gently rub your finger on the sole of your baby's foot, the fingers or toes will curl. Brothers and sisters can be shown how to slip a finger into the baby's hand to enjoy "a baby hug." This grasp reflex gradually disappears, to be replaced at about four months by a voluntary ability to reach for and hold onto people or objects. Until that age, the hands are fisted much of the time.

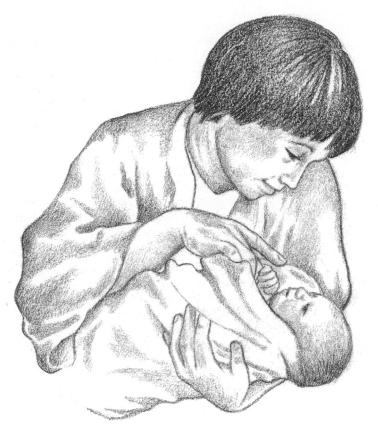

The Startle Reflex. This reflex is seen when a baby is moved rapidly, especially if the motion is downward. It is also seen in response to a baby's own crying, or to other loud sounds, and sometimes for no apparent cause. With the startle reflex, the baby's arms fly outward and the hands open, then the arms come back toward the body in a motion that looks like a hug. This reflex is seen much less frequently after the first few weeks, and it disappears after about three months. Watching the startle reflex lets us know that newborns do have a sense of equilibrium.

Swaddling the baby, holding the baby snugly, or simply holding the baby's arms and legs close to the body can help the baby contain the startle reflex. For a baby who is easily upset by the reflex, such confinement can prevent a pattern of startling, crying, then startling and crying again, until the baby is overwhelmed. Do keep in mind, though, that not all babies like to be snugly confined. See what your baby prefers.

The Fencing Reflex. You'll see the fencing, or tonic neck, reflex when your baby is lying on his or her back. When the head is turned to one side, the arm and leg on the side the infant is facing are stretched out, while the opposite arm and leg are flexed. The baby's position looks like one used in fencing. This reflex makes it easy for newborns to watch their own hand movements, so they can begin to coordinate their gaze and reach.

The Walking Reflex. When you hold your baby upright with his or her feet touching a flat surface, the baby will make stepping motions. This reflex is lost three to four weeks after birth. Once it is lost, the baby will not attempt this walking motion until he or she is ready to stand and walk.

The Crawling Reflex. When the baby is awake and on his or her tummy, press your hand against the bottoms of the baby's feet. The baby will extend his or her legs and push off against your hand. Because of this reflex, even brand-new babies are able to move fast across a flat surface. This is why it is never safe to leave a baby on a changing table or any other elevated surface.

Although newborns are quite mobile, they can't free themselves from dangerous situations. For this reason, any crib you use should be checked for safety. Each year 150 to 200 infants die in accidents involving cribs. Most injuries in infants two to nine months old are due to suffocation or entrapment of the head, arms, or legs.

Eye Reflexes. When you bring your baby to an upright position, the baby's eyes open, and the baby becomes more alert. This reflex can be used to encourage a drowsy baby to awaken enough for feedings. It can also be used to calm a baby who has been fussy

CRIB SAFETY TIPS

If you have a used crib or are considering buying one—

- Make sure it has no corner posts. Older infants can catch clothing on these.
- Check that the crib slats are no more than 2⅜ inches apart. Never put a baby in a crib that has missing slats.
- Make sure that the mattress is firm, and that it fits tightly within the crib rails, with no more than a 1-inch space (two fingers width) between the rails and the mattress.
- Assure yourself that all guide rods and support brackets are firmly in place and secure, and that no screws are missing.
- Check the locks and latches on the crib. They should be smooth, and tight enough to prevent accidental release.
- Be certain the paint used on the crib is lead-free. If it isn't, the old paint should be removed. If you're pregnant or nursing, have someone else do the stripping, preferably away from your home, or at least outside the house and away from any play or garden area. New paint should be a high-quality, lead-free enamel recommended for children's furniture. Some babies do chew on their cribs, and ingesting lead can cause brain damage.

If your crib is new, remove and discard all plastic packaging materials, including the thin plastic mattress cover. As with a used crib, check the guide rods, support brackets, locks, and latches, and make sure no screws are missing.

With any crib, new or old—

- Place the crib out of reach of any cords, electrical sockets, or other hazards.
- Keep crib rails up at all times when the baby is unattended.
- As soon as your baby can pull himself or herself up, move the mattress to the lowest position. There should be at least 22 inches between the mattress and the top of the rail.

If you plan to use a bassinet or cradle instead of a crib, many of these same safety tips will still apply.

while lying down. As the eyes open, the baby often discovers interesting things to look at, which makes life seem a little better— for a while, at least.

Reflexes That Are Permanent. Newborns have several reflexes that protect them from danger. If a bright light is flashed in a baby's face, the baby will blink. A baby will also blink if a face or object comes toward his or her face quickly. Newborns are also able to gag, cough, and sneeze, which keeps air passages clear. Babies yawn to draw in extra oxygen. They withdraw, crying, from any source of pain. They resist when they are placed in a restrained and uncomfortable position. And if a blanket covers a newborn's face, the baby will bat at it in an effort to remove it. These reflexes, of course, do not disappear but become better developed as the baby grows.

When you lay your baby face down, you will notice another protective reflex. Your baby will lift his or her head and turn it to the side. Although this helps protect the baby from smothering, a newborn cannot raise his or her head very high and cannot turn over. Any surface you place your baby face-down on should be firm enough that the baby can clear the air passages by raising his or her head. It is unsafe to have a baby sleep on a waterbed or a beanbag chair or cushion.

Your Newborn, Asleep and Awake

Babies have six states of consciousness: deep sleep, light sleep, drowsiness, a "quiet-alert" state, an "active-alert" or fussy state, and crying. Understanding how babies respond in each state, as well as how they act as they move from state to state, can help new parents recognize patterns in their babies' behavior.

The Baby's Sleep States. The need for sleep varies greatly among newborns. Some sleep only ten hours per day, whereas others sleep as much as twenty-one hours. Compared to older people, newborns have short sleep periods; they range between thirty to forty minutes and two to three hours. During any sleep period,

NEWBORN SLEEP STATES

Sleep State	How Can You Recognize This State?	What Does It Mean to You?
Deep sleep	• The baby seems completely relaxed. • Breathing is usually very regular. • The baby may occasionally startle or jerk. A startle is usually followed by a brief period of irregular breathing.	• A time to rest! • The baby is *sound* asleep. If you need to awaken the baby for feeding, wait until light sleep.
Light sleep	• The baby's breathing is less regular. • The eyes move under closed lids. The baby is dreaming! • The baby may make sucking motions. • The baby startles or moves more often, and may cry or make other noises.	• You can probably arouse the baby, if you need to, by lifting or talking to the baby or by changing his or her diaper. • Because the baby seems more active during light sleep, you may find yourself feeling on edge, expecting the baby to awaken at any moment. The baby may, however, continue sleeping. Take a nap!
Drowsiness	• The baby's eyes open and close. They may look glassy or roll upward. • The baby may fret, squirm, whimper, or wriggle.	• If the baby has been sleeping, this is a good time to prepare to feed the baby or change a diaper, to help bring the baby to a more alert state. • If the baby has been awake, this is a signal that the baby is getting sleepy.

babies alternate between deep sleep (ten to twenty minutes per cycle) and light sleep (twenty to forty minutes per cycle).

Coming Home from the Hospital. Most newborns are very sleepy for the first twenty-four to forty-eight hours after birth. If you have your baby in a hospital, it will probably be just about the time you go home that your baby will come out of the sleepy period that follows birth.

If you have looked forward to getting home so you could get some rest, you may find the first couple of days at home overwhelming. Having had little appetite in the first days, the baby may now want frequent meals. If you are breastfeeding, it may seem like the baby wants to nurse all the time. You may wonder why your baby, who seemed to sleep the time away in the hospital, now seems awake and fussy most of the time. What are you doing wrong? you wonder. Don't you have enough milk to satisfy the baby? Or can't the baby tolerate the formula you are giving?

Three big changes are at play here: a new environment to which the baby must adjust, the appearance of his or her normal appetite, and the newness of the experience for you.

If you can, take your baby and go to bed. Feed the baby whenever he or she awakens, which will probably be much more often than in the hospital. Have others take care of the cooking, phone calls, and so on.

Where Should the Baby Sleep? The answer to this question depends on two things: your preferences and your baby's preferences.

Many parents sleep with their babies in their beds, most often in the mother's arms. Across the ages and in most of the world's cultures, this has been the norm.

Other parents have the baby sleep in a bassinet, cradle, or crib in their bedrooms. This makes it easy to see the baby and be reassured that all is well without getting out of bed.

A lot of parents find that the noise and activity of a baby in light sleep make it impossible for *them* to sleep. They prefer to have the baby in a different, nearby room. The baby is still able to get their attention when they are needed.

Now, for the baby's preferences. Some babies sleep much better when next to the parent's body. Others like their own space, and sleep longer and more peacefully in their own beds. Some babies seem restless in a crib but are perfectly content in a smaller bed such as a bassinet. If you accommodate your baby's preferences, you will get more sleep, and your baby will be happier.

Sleep as a Way of Controlling the Environment. Newborns use sleep to regulate the influence of the environment on their immature nervous systems. A baby will often drift into light sleep when the environment is too stimulating, and may sleep most of the day if the house is full of visitors. Maintaining a more peaceful environment allows a baby to develop and maintain more predictable sleep-wake patterns.

Silence isn't necessary, however, for a baby to sleep. A full-term baby can easily tolerate the sounds of normal household activities, including the sounds of other children.

Sleeping Through the Night. Newborns awaken at night for many reasons. The most common is hunger. Newborns need round-the-clock nourishment. When your baby is older, he or she will begin to sleep in longer stretches. One night that stretch will seem like what you vaguely remember as "a good night's sleep." You may have gone to sleep at 11:00 and not been awakened by the baby until 5:00 A.M. Some babies regularly sleep through the night by six weeks of age, others not until three or four months or later. Even after that, all babies have periods when they awaken in the night and need their parents.

The Baby's Awake States. In the first days after birth, you may have ambivalent feelings about your baby's awake times. What does one do with an awake baby? Newborns aren't very good at entertaining themselves. For the baby, being awake usually means needing some type of attention. When the baby is asleep, you may wish the baby would wake up so the two of you could spend some time together. When the baby is awake, you might feel as if you spend much of the time trying to help the baby get back to sleep.

Gradually, you will enjoy these awake times more and more. It is during these times that you and your baby will get to know each other. Babies are more fun when you are willing to believe what you see. If you are talking to your baby and see mouth movements that look like the baby is trying to talk to you, believe it. If your baby smiles in response to your face or voice, recognize the smile as a sign of pleasure. Parents are often told newborns don't smile, or that smiles are the result of gas. Do you know anyone who smiles from gas? When the baby makes tiny coos or sounds in response to your talking, believe that these are the very beginnings of speech. When your baby frowns or looks concerned, believe in the baby's ability to show dissatisfaction. By talking to your baby with the expectation of being understood, you help your baby develop important communication skills.

Comforting a Crying Baby. Parents are still often told that responding to their babies' cries will spoil the baby. In fact, the opposite is true. Babies whose cries are answered in the first few minutes learn to cry less often. Babies whose parents do not respond to their crying, or respond slowly, end up fretting and crying more as a way to get attention.

The question for most parents, however, is not whether to help a crying baby, but how. How can you tell what your baby wants? Babies cry for many reasons, including hunger, the need to suck, gas, wet diapers, fatigue, overstimulation, and boredom. You'll soon develop a mental checklist that will enable you to identify the cause of your baby's crying, usually in seconds.

A hungry baby will root and attempt to suck on anything nearby. Offered a pacifier, the baby will look frustrated and make a very sad whimpery sound that says, "This is not what I want." Feed the baby.

A baby who is not hungry but still wants to suck may resist the breast or bottle. Help the baby find his or her fingers, or offer a

NEWBORN AWAKE STATES

Awake State	How Can You Recognize This State?	What Does It Mean to You?
Quiet-alert state	• The baby's eyes are open and shiny, the face bright, the breathing regular. • The baby stares at you or the surroundings with great interest. • The baby's body may be very still or may move in rhythm to your voice.	• When fed and comfortable, your baby will most enjoy getting to know you at this time. In the first weeks, babies spend only one to three hours a day in a quiet-alert state. This time is broken up into brief periods throughout the day and night. • You can help your newborn enter and stay in this state by talking softly and soothingly, placing your hand on the baby's arms and legs to prevent startles, and by gently rocking the baby.
Active-alert or fussy state	• The baby's eyes are open, but less focused than in the quiet-alert state. • You may notice more facial movements and squirming. • Breathing becomes more irregular. • The baby may become more sensitive to such things as too much noise or handling, or hunger.	• The baby may need your help now to stay calm. It may be time for feeding, taking a nap, or just being held quietly.
Crying	• The baby may move vigorously. • The baby's skin may be flushed. • The pitch and volume of the cry will vary depending on the need. Within a few weeks, you will be much better able to interpret your baby's cry and respond appropriately. • A few moments of crying can help the baby discharge tension or to reorganize after the work of interaction. This can help the baby move into drowsiness or sleep.	• Crying is the baby's way of saying, "I need some help." Fortunately, parents naturally want to help when they hear a baby cry. • Crying may indicate that a baby is hungry, needs to suck, has gas pain or an air bubble, has a wet or soiled diaper, is too cool or too warm, or is overstimulated, tired, bored, lonely or, occasionally, sick.

pacifier. Some babies are soothed by sucking on a parent's clean finger.

If the problem is swallowed air, help the baby burp (see page 93). Or put the baby in a position that puts pressure on the abdomen, such as face down on your lap or arm, or over your shoulder. Try gently massaging the baby's tummy.

Check for wet or soiled diapers. Many babies don't mind being wet, but some hate it.

Feel the baby's chest to tell if the baby is too warm or too cool.

Overstimulated babies need a calm environment. They may be more easily comforted if the parent doesn't talk or sing, if the lights are dim, and if the television and radio are off. Some get to sleep quicker if they're not held, but placed in their cribs and gently patted.

Tired babies often drift off to sleep with the motion of rocking, walking, or swinging. A carriage or car ride may also help the baby get to sleep.

Boredom becomes a more likely complaint as a baby gets older. A bored or lonely baby will calm when talked to or offered interesting objects to look at. He or she might enjoy a massage. Putting the baby in an infant seat in the middle of the action may be all that is needed. Or carry your baby in a sling or baby pack. As you go about your work, tell your baby what you are doing.

Colic is persistent crying for no apparent reason. Characteristic of colic are bouts of crying that begin around the third week, occur at about the same time every day (commonly, in the late afternoon or early evening, or after a night feeding), and that don't respond to any of the usual comfort measures. The crying can last two or three hours with only brief reprieves. Most babies outgrow colic by three to four months.

If your baby shows signs of colic, you may be reassured by a visit to the baby's caregiver to rule out any health problems. No one has been able to identify a definitive cause of colic. Most parents go over and over through the ways of comforting a baby already described. Any of these may calm the baby briefly, but generally the relief is only temporary.

If you have a baby with colic, you will need as much love and support as the baby needs to get through the experience. A baby who cries a lot can make a mother feel helpless, anxious, and

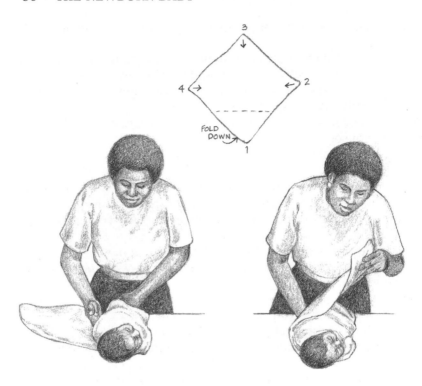

Swaddling comforts many fussy babies.

depressed. Share fussy times with your partner. Ask friends or family members who are experienced with babies to come by and give you a break. Talk out your feelings and frustrations with others. Do something nice for yourself like getting a massage or some exercise. Try not to feel personally responsible. You are not causing the colic. If you are told that a tense parent makes a colicky baby, remind yourself that just the opposite is true: a colicky baby makes a tense parent. If you find yourself worrying that you might hurt the baby because you are so frustrated, get help. Many communities have twenty-four-hour crisis-intervention phone lines (check your phone book under "Crisis Intervention" or "Crises").

If the colic does not end by the time your baby is four months old, if the crying bouts last longer than three hours, or if the baby shows any signs of illness (see pages 56–57), have your baby examined by the baby's caregiver.

Your Newborn's Temperament

Children are born with innate characteristics that influence the ways in which they interact with their world. These characteristics are evident in the earliest weeks after birth.

If you have sisters and brothers, this shouldn't surprise you. Think of how each of you is different from the others, and how each interacts with the world in a unique way. If you ask your parents about differences among you, you will probably learn that the characteristics that make each of you unique were evident very early.

What does this mean to a new parent? It means that your baby will be a unique individual from the moment of birth. If this is a second or subsequent baby, it means he or she is probably quite different from your other child or children. Here are some specific ways a baby's special characteristics may affect the early weeks of parenting:

Some newborns move slowly through the states of consciousness, give their parents clear signals about their needs, and are comforted fairly easily. Other babies leap from one state of consciousness to another, for example, from sleeping right into crying. Parents learn to respond quickly to these babies at their first stirrings, and skip diaper changes until after the babies have nursed or calmed down.

Some babies' signals about their needs are unclear. This makes it hard for parents to follow a baby's lead in an interaction or to know when a change of activity is needed. Parents of these babies need a lot of support as they learn to understand a baby's messages. If you have a very unpredictable baby, you might ask for help from a specialist in child development, especially one who has a particular interest in infants. You may be able to get a referral from your baby's caregiver. Your local hospital, especially if it has a newborn intensive care unit, may have an infant development specialist on staff. This person can help you learn to understand your baby's way of relating to the world.

Some babies are hypersensitive; they overreact to almost any stimulus. Their parents learn to move these babies slowly and speak to them softly. They also avoid doing too many things at once, including things to comfort their babies, like holding, rocking, and singing. These parents have to learn to plan more time for everything so their babies don't get upset by too much happening at once.

Many babies show signs of distress when handed over to an unfamiliar person. It takes courage, but sometimes you have to tell friends—or even grandparents—that your baby needs time just to watch and listen to a person before feeling comfortable in that person's arms. Babies as young as two weeks old can show a preference in who holds them.

One of the most important things you can do as a parent is to value your baby's unique approach to life and to adjust your parenting style to fit the baby's temperament. If you can do this, you and your baby will achieve what two writers have called "goodness of fit."[5] When there is goodness of fit between a baby's way of relating to the world and the world's way of responding to the baby, he or she grows into a happy, healthy child and adult.

Some Basics about Feeding

Expectant parents know they will have a lot to learn after their babies arrive. They know it will take time to feel confident about diapering, bathing, and soothing a baby. Most have been told that feeding, too, will be a learning experience. It is not until after the birth, however, that the true meaning of this is clear. Parents often say they had not anticipated that the baby, too, would need to learn to feed. Also unanticipated is the profound concern parents have that their babies be adequately nourished.

Even as adults, many people are greeted by their mothers with the questions "Are you hungry? Do you want to eat?" These are questions you will find yourself asking your baby. It is natural for you to feel somewhat anxious when the baby's answers are not as clear as you might like. Following are some basics about feeding that can guide you as you gain experience.

The Newborn's Need for Nourishment. A healthy full-term baby is well able to survive a period of learning how to feed. Many newborns show few signs of hunger in the first twenty-four to forty-eight hours after birth. Put to breast or offered formula, they suck for a few minutes and drift off to sleep, seemingly satisfied. Newborns have fluid reserves at birth, which is one reason they look a bit puffy. These reserves provide the baby a safety net, and should provide you some reassurance that your baby will not be harmed either by lack of interest or limited skill during the first several feedings. Expect it will take some time before both you and the baby are at ease with the feeding experience.

Getting Advice about Feeding. Ask for help when you need it; don't wait until you and the baby are frustrated by several poor feedings. Early help can prevent problems later.

Expect conflicting advice about feeding—from friends, family members, nurses, doctors, and midwives. There is no one right way to feed a baby. Follow advice that makes sense to you and that works. Ignore the other advice.

If you are breastfeeding, you'll likely get the best advice from a breastfeeding counselor who can observe you and your baby during a feeding. Many hospitals now have lactation consultants on staff. If yours doesn't, your baby's caregiver may be able to refer you to a lactation specialist. Or contact La Leche League, a volunteer organization that provides a range of services to breastfeeding mothers. To find out about groups in your community, look up *La Leche* in the white pages of your phone book or call the national office at 800-LA LECHE. In some cities, the Nursing Mothers Counsel also provides breastfeeding advice; again, check the white pages of your phone book.

If you are formula feeding, a hospital nurse, your baby's caregiver, or a visiting nurse may be helpful in finding solutions to any problems you and the baby are having.

Feeding When the Baby Is Hungry. Babies do best if they are fed when hungry, rather than on a predetermined schedule. Signs that a newborn is hungry include a distinctive short and rhythmic cry, rooting, batting the cheek or ear with a hand, and sucking on whatever is handy.

How often a newborn gets hungry depends on many things, including birth weight and length, growth spurts, metabolism (how quickly the baby digests food), and whether the baby is breast-or formula-fed. Since the combination of these varies from baby to baby, the best rule for the parents is to watch the baby, not the clock, to determine when it's time for a feeding. A possible exception to this is a baby who regularly goes more than four hours between formula feedings or more than three to four hours between breast feedings. To assure adequate weight gain, these babies may need to be awakened for feedings. If you want to awaken your baby for a feeding, watch for signs of light sleep (see page 80).

In the first several weeks, breastfed babies generally want to nurse about every one to three hours during the daytime and every three to four hours at night. Formula-fed babies usually feed about every two and a half to four hours during the daytime and every three to four hours at night. At first, of course, most babies do not know the difference between day and night. After the first month, when the baby is awake more hours of the day, more frequent feedings during the day eventually help babies adjust their internal clocks so the longer stretches between feedings occur at night.

All babies have times when they need to eat more frequently than usual. This often happens at about three weeks, six weeks, and three months—ages at which most babies go through growth spurts. If you are formula feeding, at these times you will need to increase the amount of formula you offer. If you are breastfeeding, you may feel as if you are nursing nonstop for a day or two. The frequent feedings will increase your milk production to the level needed to feed a bigger baby. If you can, take a break from other responsibilities at these times; ask for extra support from family members.

Your Baby's Feeding Style. Babies differ not only in how often they want their meals, but in how much time they spend at each meal and in their style of feeding.

On average, babies take about twenty to forty minutes to finish a feeding. Many, however, take an hour or even more.

Some newborns drift off to sleep once initial hunger is satisfied. A sleepy baby may wake up and resume feeding if you switch to the other breast, burp the baby, or change the baby's diaper. But some babies, if prodded, will get upset, and cry rather than continue to feed. Such a baby may end up having shorter feedings— of, say, ten minutes each—every hour to one and one-half hours. This can be because the baby was underweight at birth and needs to catch up. It can also be simply because this infant is the sort who will grow into a child and adult who eats frequent small meals throughout the day. In either case, with such a baby you will end up having an impressive milk supply, because the frequent feedings trigger increased milk production. You will need to take great care of yourself and get a lot of extra help for the first few weeks.

Some babies are very tidy eaters; their suck and swallow reflexes are well developed from day one. Others are noisy and somewhat messy, they choke and sputter, or swallow a lot of air, and need frequent burping.

If your baby often chokes at the beginning of a feeding, this may be because your milk sprays when it lets down (see page 13), which makes it hard for your newborn to control the flow. If the baby gets upset at this, calm the baby and try again. In just a matter of days, the baby will be better able to handle the flow of milk, or may simply learn to pull off the breast and let the milk spray. Keep a cloth diaper or towel handy to catch the spray.

If you are bottle feeding, sputtering and choking may be signs that the hole in the nipple is too large. When you turn the bottle upside down, milk should come out one drop at a time, not in a stream. If the milk streams out, use a different nipple.

Sometimes the holes in bottle nipples are too small. If the baby has a hard time getting milk out of the bottle, try another nipple.

Some babies cannot tolerate a lot of distraction during feedings. They may need to be fed in a quiet place away from most of the household's activity. Retreating to a quiet spot can make feeding a more relaxed time for you as well as your baby.

It may be hard to believe now, but feeding your baby will be much easier within only a few weeks. Have confidence! Any anxiety you feel is simply evidence of what a great parent you want to be. Your baby can't ask for much more than that!

Some Things Your Baby May Not Tolerate. Another way babies differ is in their sensitivity to foods—in their diets or, if they are breastfed, in their mothers' diets. A breastfed baby may be fussy or have gas for as long as a day after the mother has eaten broccoli, onions, garlic, cabbage, brussel sprouts, beans, cauliflower, or too much fresh fruit. If your baby seems to react to one of these foods, you will probably want to eat that food in only small amounts, at least until the baby is a few weeks older.

Occasionally, a breastfed baby has an allergic reaction to a food in the mother's diet. Signs of allergy may include frequent and greenish stools, gas, a stuffy nose, a rash, and vomiting. If these symptoms occur, you may consider eliminating from your diet foods that most frequently cause reactions: milk and milk products, citrus fruits, tomatoes, pineapples, chocolate, eggs, and peanuts. Kathleen Huggins, author of *The Nursing Mother's Companion*, suggests eliminating all of these foods for one week, then adding each food back into the diet at one-week intervals.[6] (If you eliminate milk and milk products from your diet, ask your doctor or midwife for advice regarding calcium supplements.)

Your breastfed baby may do better if you limit caffeine, which is found in coffee, tea, cola drinks, and chocolate. Artificial sweeteners may also cause problems in some babies.

If you are formula feeding, your baby may be able to tolerate any infant formula. Or you may need to try two or three different formulas before you find one that suits the baby. Formulas are not all the same—but the differences among them are fairly complex. Ask your baby's caregiver to guide you in decisions about choosing and switching formulas. Once you have found a formula that is satisfactory for your baby, don't switch to another brand.

Babies can react to substances in the air as well as to those in food. Not only do breastfed babies of smokers ingest nicotine, but both breast- and formula-fed babies suffer in smoke-filled rooms. If you used to smoke, you probably worked hard to quit or cut down before or during pregnancy. If so, don't start again! If you are still working to kick the habit, at least never smoke around your baby. Ask others not to, either.

Burping. Most babies, whether breast-or formula-fed, need to be burped. You can burp a baby by sitting the baby upright, laying the baby on your shoulder, or laying the baby over your lap. A baby who stops feeding and starts fussing may be signaling a need to be burped. For most babies, being burped about halfway through a feeding and at the end is enough. Others may need to be burped before a feeding and more often during the feeding. Some babies take in very little air during a feeding so may not burp all that readily. Two or three minutes is probably an adequate amount of time to try to "bubble" a baby.

When burping in the middle of a feeding, watch for signs that the baby will tolerate a break, such as slowing down or drifting into sleep. If you are breastfeeding, the natural time to burp the baby is when he or she has finished at one breast. If your baby consistently gets upset when you stop feeding to burp, skip the burping. Crying will only add to any air in the baby's stomach.

Spitting Up. Most babies spit up small amounts of milk, usually after feedings or when they are burped. The amount may sometimes seem more than small, especially when you are on your sixth change of clothes for the day. Keep a cloth diaper handy for wipe-ups or to cover your shoulder. Spitting up probably prevents the baby's small stomach from becoming overly full.

Spitting up is different from vomiting. Vomiting usually involves a much larger quantity of milk, which comes out with some force. If your baby vomits during or after two feedings in twenty-four hours, contact your baby's caregiver.

Supplementing with Cow's Milk and Solid Foods. Throughout the first year, babies should be given either breast milk or infant formula. Most caregivers advise against giving other forms of milk before one year of age. You should consult with your baby's caregiver before introducing cow's milk into your baby's diet. When you do introduce cow's milk, use milk with at least 2 percent fat content. Babies need milk fat in their diets.

Babies can thrive on breast milk or formula alone for at least the first six months after birth. There is no need to introduce solid foods before your baby is six months old. Many parents are told that introducing solids helps a baby sleep through the night, but research has shown this not to be true.[7]

An ideal time to introduce your baby to solid foods is when he or she begins to reach for food on the table. By then, the baby should be able to sit upright in a chair and take food off of a spoon. Introducing solid foods too soon means spending a lot of time putting food in the baby's mouth just to have the baby push it out again—a tiresome process for both parent and baby.

Getting Breastfeeding off to a Good Start

Some Facts about Breast Milk. Human breast milk offers the newborn all the nutrients needed in the ideal amounts, and the makeup of the milk changes in response to the baby's changing needs. Breast milk also contains antibodies that protect the baby against infection. Because of this, breastfed babies are generally sick less than bottle-fed babies; they have fewer cases of diarrhea, ear infection, and respiratory illnesses, including pneumonia. Breast milk is easily digested, so stomach upsets occur less often in breastfed babies. And breast milk, unlike formula, contains the long-chain fatty acids necessary for optimal brain growth.

Positioning the Baby at the Breast. Learning to position your baby at the breast may seem like a big deal at first, but soon it will be second nature. Your goal is to help the baby latch on to your breast in a way that enables the baby to milk the breast efficiently and avoids trauma to your nipple. The baby is properly latched on to the breast when the gums are around the areola. For this to happen, the baby has to have a wide-open mouth when brought to the breast, and his or her nose and chin must touch the breast. In this position the baby can compress the milk sinuses under the areola and draw the milk out.

A rule of thumb is that the baby's suckling should not hurt, though you may feel some tugging sensations as the baby begins the feeding. If you feel pain beyond that, slip your finger into the baby's mouth to break the suction, and start again.

Your baby can latch on correctly from a variety of positions. For the first few feedings, you might find it easier if both you and your baby go topless, so your clothing doesn't get in the way.

The cradle hold. This is the classic nursing position.

- Sit upright with your back well supported.
- Hold your baby in one of your arms, tummy to tummy, the baby's head resting in the bend in your elbow. You can tuck the baby's lower arm out of the way.
- Use your other hand to lift and support your breast. That hand should be held like a backwards *C*, with thumb on top and fingers under the breast. Keep your fingers well behind the areola.
- Stimulate the baby's rooting reflex by touching the baby's lower lip with your nipple.
- As soon as the baby opens the mouth wide, lift your breast to align with the baby's open mouth and quickly pull the baby in to the breast. (Don't lean into the baby. Your back will feel better if you pull the baby into you.)

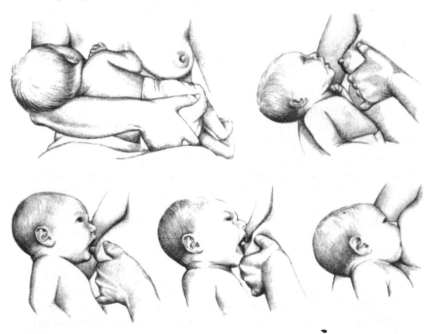

If the baby has the areola correctly in the mouth and has started suckling, you can relax your arm under the baby so his or her nose doesn't press into your breast. You may or may not need to continue supporting your breast with the other hand.

If the baby has not latched on correctly, slip your finger into the baby's mouth, break the suction, and try again.

The football hold. This position is ideal for a woman who has had a cesarean, because there is no pressure against the incision.

- Sit upright with your back well supported.
- Put a pillow at your side. Place your baby on it, with the baby's buttocks at about the level of your waist, so the baby is facing you. Support the baby's head with your hand and his or her back with your arm.
- Use your other hand to lift and support your breast, as for the cradle hold.
- Touch the baby's mouth with your nipple. When the mouth opens wide, pull the baby quickly to the breast.

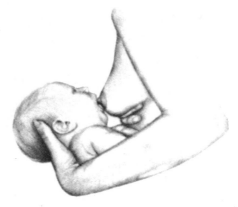

The side-lying position. This is a favorite position of mothers who like to nurse their babies in bed. It is also comfortable for women who have had cesareans.

- Lie on your side with pillows beneath your shoulder and head.
- Lay your baby on his or her side, with the baby's head facing your breast. If you need to, place a pillow under the baby to raise the baby to a comfortable level.

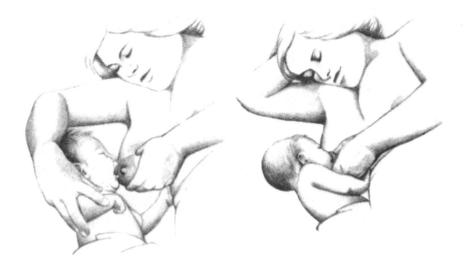

- Lift the breast, and touch the baby's mouth with your nipple. Using your other hand, move the baby onto the breast as the baby's mouth opens wide.

Other Breastfeeding Tips.

- Listen for swallowing while your baby nurses. This tells you the baby is taking milk. If you hear clicking sounds, the baby is probably only on the nipple. Take the baby off the breast and start again.
- Encourage the baby to take both breasts at each feeding. Nurse the baby on the first breast until the baby slows down, stops swallowing, or goes to sleep. Burp the baby, or just turn the baby around onto your other arm. The baby will probably wake up and resume nursing.
- Try to start each feeding with the breast you ended with last time—especially if the baby did not completely empty that breast.
- Wash your hands before handling your breasts, especially in the hospital, where there are more dangerous germs than in your own home.
- Wash your breasts with water only. Soap is unnecessary and could dry out the areola.

Is the Baby Getting Enough? You'll know your baby is getting enough milk in the first weeks if—

• The baby is nursing at least eight times in every twenty-four hours.
• You can hear swallowing sounds throughout the feeding.
• The baby wets at least eight diapers a day by the fifth day.
• The baby has yellowish stools each day after the fourth or fifth day.
• The baby has regained his or her birth weight by two weeks of age, and has gained at least five ounces per week thereafter.

Sore Nipples. Although sore nipples can take the fun out of breastfeeding for a while, they *do* heal. The best treatment will depend on the cause.

Cracked and bleeding nipples. Cracking or bleeding of the nipple is usually caused by the baby's latching on incorrectly. For this problem, try the following measures:

• Express a small amount of milk (see page 100) before putting the baby to the breast. This can soften the areola enough that the baby grasps it better.
• Start each feeding on the breast with the least sore nipple.
• Select a position that gives you good control of the baby's head. The football hold is often ideal for assuring a correct latch.
• Be persistent in getting the baby to latch on correctly. Take the baby off immediately if the latch doesn't feel right. Do this as many times as needed to get the baby on the breast right.
• Relieve the pain of nursing on the sore nipple by taking acetaminophen thirty minutes before a feeding or by holding ice against the nipple just before nursing.
• Nurse for shorter periods of time more often—say, for ten minutes every hour. Massage the breast while nursing so it empties faster.
• Before taking the baby off the breast, always release the baby's suction by putting your little finger in the corner of the baby's mouth.

- At the end of the feeding rub a few drops of expressed milk over the nipple. The milk may help it heal.
- Air-dry your breast between feedings. If you are wearing a nursing bra, leave the flaps down.
- Avoid nipple creams or oils, which can cause an allergic reaction characterized by reddening and a burning sensation.

If these measures don't help, try to get guidance from a lactation consultant.

Thrush infection. Thrush is a yeast infection in a baby's mouth (see page 65). It can result from the baby's exposure to a vaginal yeast infection during birth, or from antibiotics given to either the mother or the baby. During nursing it can spread to the mother's nipples, making them itch, burn, or flake.

Both the mother's nipples and the baby's mouth need to be treated with medication to overcome this infection. Contact your doctor or midwife or the baby's caregiver for prescriptions and guidance. To prevent reinfection, launder bras or nursing pads and dispose of pacifiers used before or during treatment.

Expressing and Storing Breast Milk. You will want to express your milk when your breasts feel overly full or when you wish to collect milk to save for feedings when you are away. You can express milk by hand or by using a breast pump. Hand expression, once learned, is easy, and can be more efficient than using a manual pump.

If you are collecting milk to feed your baby later, the process will take about fifteen to twenty minutes. You can collect the milk in a clean bowl, but it is best stored in a hard plastic container or plastic bottles. Follow these steps:

- Wash your hands and any container you will be using.
- Position your thumb above the nipple, and your first two fingers below it, 1 to 1½ inches from the nipple.
- Push against the chest wall.
- Roll your thumb and fingers forward at the same time, keeping your fingers behind the nipple.

- Repeat this motion a few times, then rotate your hand a bit and repeat the motion a few times more. Continue this way, gradually rotating around the areola. To empty all your milk reservoirs, switch hands and repeat the process.
- Repeat these steps on the other breast. Then repeat the whole process for another two to three minutes at each breast.

Massaging your breast or just having your baby nearby may help stimulate your milk to let down. Massage your breast with gentle patting motions, much as in a breast self-exam, not by squeezing the breast or sliding the fingers down or around the breast, which could cause bruising.

Expressed breast milk can be stored in the refrigerator for twenty-four hours, in the freezer compartment of a refrigerator for two weeks, or in a deep freeze (with a temperature below 0° Fahrenheit) for six months. Label milk with the date it was collected, and use the oldest milk first. Cool freshly expressed breast milk in the refrigerator before adding it to a bottle of frozen stored milk.

TIPS ON FEEDING STORED BREAST MILK

- **Thaw frozen milk in the refrigerator for a few hours before the feeding.**
- **Shake the bottle of breast milk before pouring a portion into another bottle or feeding the milk directly to the baby.**
- **Warm the milk by running warm water over the bottle for a few minutes. Be careful not to overheat the milk. Always test the temperature by sprinkling a few drops on your wrist before feeding the baby.**
- **Do not heat breast milk in a microwave oven. Doing so could destroy nutrients and heat the milk unevenly, possibly leading to burns.**
- **After the feeding, dispose of any milk left in the bottle.**

Getting Bottle Feeding off to a Good Start

Some Facts about Formula. Infant formula is the best substitute for breast milk throughout a baby's first year. Most formula is made of cow's milk supplemented with animal and vegetable fats and oils. Soy-based formula is also available, for the one in ten babies who have difficulty digesting formula made with cow's milk or who develop an allergy to cow's milk formula. For infants who cannot tolerate either of these kinds of formula, or who have an illness such as PKU or galactosemia (see page 49), there are specially developed formulas that meet their nutritional requirements.

In the United States, the Food and Drug Administration analyzes formula for twenty-four essential nutrients and other properties. This review process provides parents with assurance that major brands of formula meet government standards—and, therefore, the infant's basic nutritional needs. The Consumers Union recommends that parents use only major formula brands, preferably those recommended by their babies' caregivers. Less common formulas, such as some sold in health food stores, may not have all the nutrients essential for healthy development.[8]

The First Feeding. In the hospital, a nurse will provide ready-to-feed infant formula when you are ready for the first feeding. Generally, the milk is fed at room temperature.

- Cradle your baby in your arm with the head slightly elevated. You will be more comfortable if you use pillows to support your arm.
- Stroke the baby's lips with the nipple of the bottle. The baby will open his or her mouth. Glide the nipple into the baby's mouth, making certain the tongue is below the nipple, not above. The baby should have a sealed grasp all around the nipple.
- Keep the bottle at a tilt so the nipple is filled with fluid at all times.
- If the baby stops sucking, you can rotate the nipple in the mouth to encourage the baby to continue. When the baby pulls away from the bottle or falls asleep, you can assume the baby is full for the time being.

Feeding as Part of a Loving Relationship. Formula feeding can support the bond between parent and infant in the same way breastfeeding can. Always hold your baby next to your body during feedings. Never prop a bottle. Not only could this make the baby choke, but it would deprive both you and the baby of closeness during feeding time. If you feel comfortable doing so, feed your baby when you are both undressed, the baby's skin against yours. This direct physical contact helps meet the baby's need for touching. A blanket over both of you will keep the baby warm.

Switch arms during feedings. Moving the baby from one side to the other promotes more symmetrical muscular development, including the development of eye muscles. Babies spend a lot of time gazing at their parents during feedings.

Bottles and Nipples. An incredible variety of nipples and bottles is available. Select unbreakable bottles that are easy to see through and keep clean. Eight-ounce-bottles may be more economical than the 4-ounce size, which within weeks may prove too small. You will probably need eight bottles a day. The shape of the nipples

you use is a matter of personal preference—yours and your baby's. There are no documented benefits of one nipple over another.

Choosing and Preparing Formula. Your baby's caregiver can tell you about formula brands and assist you in deciding on the best formula for your baby. Don't assume that the formula the hospital gives your baby is the one you should use. Hospitals are given formula by formula companies, who use this as a method of advertising.

When you shop for formula, check the expiration date on the container. Do not buy or use formula that is outdated. Also, do not buy formula in a container that is damaged in any way.

Almost all formula companies provide their formula in three forms: ready-to-feed, concentrate, and powdered. Each is prepared differently. Ready-to-feed is just that; water should not be added. Both formula concentrate and powdered formula are mixed with water. Read the directions on the can or package carefully. Too little water could cause diarrhea and dehydration; too much water could cause malnourishment.

When you prepare formula and bottles, cleanliness is essential. If your baby's caregiver recommends sterilization, follow the directions on the formula label. Whether or not you sterilize, these measures are important:

- Wash bottles and nipples in hot, soapy water, and rinse them thoroughly before each use. If you rinse the bottles and nipples immediately after using them, they will be easier to clean. You can wash the bottles in a dishwasher, but wash the nipples by hand, forcing soapy water through the nipple openings. Let the nipples air-dry. Discard nipples if they get sticky, dry, or cracked.
- Boil water for at least five minutes, then let it cool before mixing it with formula.
- Wash your hands before mixing the formula.
- If you are using liquid formula, shake the can.
- Wash the top of the formula can before opening it. Open it with a clean can opener. Be certain all measuring equipment is thoroughly clean.
- Once the formula is prepared, give it to the baby or refrigerate it immediately.

• If the formula has been refrigerated, you may prefer to warm it slightly by placing it in a pan of hot water. Test the temperature by letting it drip onto your wrist. Do not heat formula in a microwave oven. The formula would heat unevenly, and so could burn the baby's mouth.

Storing Formula. You will probably find it easiest to prepare a day's supply of formula at a time, especially if you are using concentrate. Store prepared formula in tightly sealed bottles in your refrigerator until you are ready to use it. Discard any formula that has not been used within forty-eight hours. Do not freeze formula. If it freezes in the back of the refrigerator, discard it.

Opened cans of formula concentrate can be stored in the refrigerator, covered, for up to forty-eight hours. Formula powder can be stored at room temperature, covered, for up to one month.

After feeding your baby, always discard any formula left in the bottle, since bacteria breeds quickly in formula. If you find you are discarding a lot of formula, put smaller amounts in each bottle.

Is the Baby Getting Enough? In the first days, newborns take from 1 to 3 ounces of formula about seven or eight times a day. They gradually increase their intake after that. By the time the baby is three or four months old, he or she will probably take 6 or 7 ounces of formula four or five times a day. You'll know your baby is getting enough formula if he or she sucks vigorously during feedings, seems contented afterward, and is gaining weight appropriately.

Bathing Your Baby

Some newborns enjoy baths, but many don't. Fortunately, new babies don't need a lot of bathing; twice weekly baths are usually plenty. By the time your baby is active enough to need more frequent bathing, he or she will probably love bathtime.

The Sponge Bath. Give sponge baths until the baby's cord falls off and, if the baby was circumcised, the penis has healed. A lot of parents continue sponge baths for a few weeks after this just because they are easier than tub baths. If your baby gets upset during a sponge bath, you can easily stop at any point to offer comfort.

Sponge-bathe your baby on a surface covered with a blanket or towel, in a draft-free room. Have at hand a basin of warm water (check the temperature by dipping your elbow into it) and a clean washcloth and towel. Soap is not necessary at this age; it would dry the baby's skin. If you want to wash the baby's hair, use a "no-tears" shampoo.

You can wash the baby's hair before undressing the baby. Hold your baby like a football with his or her head over the basin of water. Moisten the hair, apply a tiny amount of shampoo, lather, and rinse. Dry the hair by gently patting the head with a clean towel.

Some babies develop a scaly layer of skin on the scalp, called *cradle cap*. If you notice signs of this, put a little baby oil on the affected areas before washing the hair. This will help loosen the flakes. (Combing or brushing the baby's hair—regardless of how little there is—will also help control cradle cap.)

Wipe one eye with a corner of a wet washcloth, then the other eye with a fresh corner.

Now wash the ears, the rest of the face, and the neck, removing any lint in the skin folds of the neck. Gently pat dry.

Take off the baby's top. Wash the chest, the underarms, the arms, and the hands. Pat dry, and cover the baby's chest and abdomen with a blanket.

Remove the baby's diaper. Wash the genitals, legs, and feet. Take care to get the skin folds clean. Pat dry.

Place the baby tummy down. Wash the back and buttocks. Pat dry.

The Full Bath. When the baby is ready for a full bath, it may be easiest if you bathe together. Make sure the water is warm but not hot, then have another adult hand you the baby as you sit in the tub. Many babies find baths much more pleasant this way. At the end of the bath, your helper should take the baby, towel ready, before you get up.

You can also bathe your baby in an infant bath tub or a clean

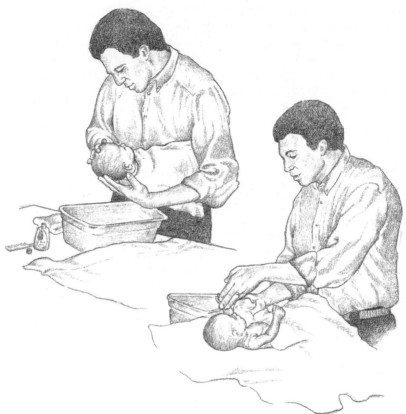

Washing the baby's hair; wiping the baby's eyes.

kitchen sink with several inches of warm water. (Or you can use the bathtub, but even if you have a special bath chair you'll need to keep one hand on the baby at all times. Make sure there is nothing in the tub that could injure the baby, such as soap, shampoo, or a razor, and *never* leave your baby alone in the tub.) Keep the room draft-free.

Again, wash the baby's face and, if you like, the hair before undressing the baby. Holding the baby in the water as shown, wash the front from top to bottom. Soap isn't needed, but if you use it rinse it off well. Turn the baby over on your arm, and wash

A bath in the kitchen sink.

the back side from top to bottom. Wrap the baby in a towel, and pat the baby dry.

Caring for the Umbilical Cord Stump. Keep the cord stump as dry as possible until it falls off, between one and three weeks after birth. Fold the diaper down under the cord stump after each diaper change, and don't give a tub bath until the cord has fallen off. You can help the cord dry out by using a sterile cotton ball or gauze pad, soaked in alcohol, to wipe around the stump with each diaper change. If you notice redness or oozing around the stump, or a bad odor from it, contact your baby's caregiver.

Diapering Your Baby

There are so many diapering methods and diapering supplies and diapering debates today that new parents can feel overwhelmed. If possible, go shopping with an experienced parent who can give you advice on the necessary supplies and the best products.

Your Own Cloth Diapers. Owning and washing your baby's diapers is the least expensive method of diapering your baby and the most "environmentally friendly." You will need:

- *Four dozen cloth diapers.* Prefolded diapers are easiest to use.
- *Two or three pairs of diaper pins or clips.* Storing diaper pins poked into a bar of soap keeps their points smooth so they slide into the diaper. Clips take practice to use, but some parents prefer them. Diapers or clips may be unnecessary if your diaper covers, or the diapers themselves, have Velcro closures.
- *Four to six diaper covers.* Wool covers absorb moisture; plastic or nylon pants keep moisture in, but can increase diaper rash.
- *A diaper pail.* Look for one that you can open with your foot and that has strong handles for carrying to the washing machine. Since the water in the pail can be a hazard for toddlers in your home, keep the pail in a safe place. Deodorant cakes, sold with some diaper pails, can also be a hazard to small children, and so are not recommended.

Following is a standard method for laundering cloth diapers:

- Put one to two gallons of water in the pail; add borax powder, if you like—1 teaspoon per gallon or according to instructions on the box.
- Rinse soiled diapers and wring them out before putting them in the diaper pail.
- When you're ready to do the laundry, pour all the contents of the pail into the washing machine. Set the machine on spin, and spin out the excess moisture.
- Set the machine on hot wash–cold rinse. Add a low-suds detergent and, if you wish, more borax powder.
- When the cycle is complete, rinse again, using cold water.
- Dry in a hot dryer or on a clothesline in the sun.

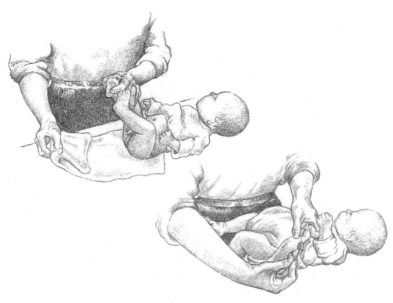

For a better fit and extra absorbency, fold the diaper down in front if your baby is a boy, in back if your baby is a girl.

Most diaper covers can be washed with diapers but last longer if you hang them out to dry.

Diaper Services. Your community may have a service that delivers clean diapers, and takes the used ones away, once a week. If so, using this service is an option worth exploring, at least for the first few weeks. Using a diaper service is more expensive than buying and washing your own diapers, but it is usually about half the cost of buying disposables, and is very convenient besides. Most diaper services can provide a wide variety of diaper types and can specially launder a baby's diapers if the baby's skin is particularly sensitive.

Most services also provide diaper pails. You still need to purchase diaper covers.

If you are considering a diaper service, find out how the diapers are washed, handled, and stored. In many communities, no health agency regulates diaper services to assure sanitation. You might call your health department to find out about local guidelines and standards.

Disposable Diapers. Disposable diapers are convenient but also expensive. And many parents worry about their environmental effects, including the depletion of our forests to produce the cellulose in them, and the great quantities of solid waste they become.

Many parents use disposables in the first few weeks to limit their work loads, then switch to cloth diapers. If you decide to use disposables, you'll need four to six dozen a week.

Diaper Rash. Regardless of what type of diapers you use, washing the baby's bottom with each diaper change will help keep the skin healthy. Use a clean, damp washcloth without soap. Although store-bought diaper wipes are convenient for travel, I don't recommend them for everyday care since they irritate many babies' skin.

Even with careful cleaning, mild diaper rash may appear. This looks like chafing; the skin is reddened but has no raised areas. You can reduce the chance of diaper rash by changing diapers promptly. Disposable diapers may feel dry after a baby urinates, but ammonia in the urine still affects the skin, so change the diaper at least every three hours.

Exposing the skin to air for brief periods each day also helps prevent or heal diaper rash. After the first two to three weeks, your baby probably won't mind being uncovered. Then you can place the baby, bare-bottomed, on a waterproof pad covered by a couple of diapers. You can also use a zinc oxide ointment on the skin, but I don't recommend cornstarch or other powders. Cornstarch may serve as a breeding ground for bacteria, and talcum powder is easily breathed into the baby's lungs—and yours. If you do use it, shake the powder into your hand, away from the baby's face.

Contact your baby's caregiver if your baby develops a diaper rash that has raised areas, looks raw, has pimples that develop white heads or blisters, or does not get better with home treatment in a couple of days. A common cause of persistent diaper rash is an allergic reaction to a substance that comes in contact with the baby's skin. The offending substance may be a component of disposable diapers, plastic pants, detergents, powders, lotions, fabric softeners, baby wipes, or perfumes used in any baby product that touches the skin. A yeast infection can also cause persistent diaper rash. This type of rash, which may look like a patch of red dots or a mild burn, must be treated with medication.

The Newborn Family

Keeping Family Relationships Strong

One of a couple's major concerns during pregnancy may be how the new baby will affect their relationship with each other. Couples find the postpartum period easier when—

- Both parents are prepared to make their own relationship secondary to building a relationship with the baby during the first few months.
- Communication is open, thoughtful, and ongoing.
- Sexual needs are discussed and met in a mutually satisfying and respectful way.

Expectant parents are often told that one of the most important gifts they can give their child is their own healthy, loving relationship. This is true, but a qualifier must be added: The birth of a baby brings real changes in a couple's relationship. A common question of expectant and new parents is "How long before things return to normal?" If *normal* means the way things were before the pregnancy, the answer is never.

All thriving relationships are dynamic—that is, they evolve as the individuals in them mature and develop. Adults expect and encourage developmental change in their children. They often forget to expect it in themselves. All healthy adults go through bursts in maturational development, which are driven as much by internal rhythms as external events. The addition of a child to the family is one of the greatest developmental opportunities a human can experience.

For parents as well as children, change usually means hard work. Both parents may have moments when they find themselves saying, "Parenthood is great, but I didn't realize I would have to give up my relationship with my partner to experience it."

At least two big changes have happened. One is that you have a new responsibility—taking care of a baby—that requires most of your energy. Meeting your own basic needs, for food, sleep, and shelter, plus those of the baby's uses up almost every minute of the day for at least the first two months of a newborn's life.

The other, and perhaps bigger, change is that you are falling in love. Your baby is pulling you into a love affair that has to be experienced to be believed. This love affair is the work of attachment. Babies and "newborn parents" are designed for this event.

When my sons were teenagers, they used to call falling in love being "whupped." They or fellow teens were whupped when they could not think of anything but the object of their love, and started neglecting their friends, their studies, their families, sports, and everything else. This behavior might not be entirely healthy for teens, but for parents and babies, who will be committed to each other for a lifetime, being whupped is absolutely essential. Healthy families are formed when parents clear a temporary space in their lives to allow this love affair to happen.

So how long will it be until things return to what might be called "the new normal?" The most intense period of forming the parent-child relationship lasts five or six months, after which both parents and baby start to show greater interest in the rest of the world. As your life settles into what might be called "the new normal," you may feel as if you are emerging from a cocoon. The rest of this section is about practical things you can do to take care of your relationship during this critical time of metamorphosis.

Patterns of Communication. Couples tend to communicate in the patterns they learned from their parents. If these patterns were open, thoughtful, and ongoing in both your families of origin, communication between you and your mate is probably the same. But if the communication patterns between you aren't so good, here are some ways to improve them:

- Become a great listener. When your mate is talking to you, focus your attention on what is being said rather than on what your response will be.
- Use "I messages" rather than "you messages" to communicate your needs, wants, and feelings. For example, "I need to have more time with you to keep our relationship strong" states both what you need and why. In contrast, "You don't pay attention to me anymore" is accusatory and provides no information for problem solving.
- Be forgiving about things said during vulnerable times of the day (or night). One wise couple had a rule that neither parent would be held accountable for anything said before 9:00 in the morning. These parents realized that since neither were "morning people," this was a time when communication tended to break down. Their agreement allowed them to focus their energy on "real" problems when they arose, rather than wasting time on matters more of biorhythms than true feelings.

As you learned your parents' communication patterns, so your children will learn yours. From the moment of birth (and perhaps before), children are observing how to communicate. If the communication patterns in your household need work, start that work now.

Postpartum Sexual Adjustment. It is safe to have sexual intercourse after childbirth when there is no longer any discharge from the vagina (see "Lochia," pages 5–6) and when any tear or episiotomy is healed and no longer tender. For some women this means about three to four weeks after childbirth. For others, it means a few months after childbirth. The decision to resume having sexual intercourse, of course, involves much more than physical recovery from childbirth. It involves emotional readiness on the part of both the woman and her mate. The timing of emotional readiness varies as much as that of physical readiness. Attention to both nurtures loving relationships. (For information on birth control, see page 116.)

A number of factors affect both sexual needs and desires after a baby's birth:

Fatigue. Often, sexual desire simply cannot compete with a desire for sleep. When this is the case, a nap might be the best kind of foreplay. For some parents, the morning or the middle of the day is a better time for lovemaking than bedtime or the middle of the night.

Pain during sex. Some women find sex painful after childbirth. There can be several reasons for this. The site of a vaginal tear or episiotomy can remain tender for a few weeks or even months after childbirth. Taking a warm bath before sex and using a sterile lubricant during sex can help. These measures also help if the perineum feels tight. Massaging the perineum, by gliding one or two fingers back and forth across the tight tissues, may increase its elasticity.

This may be a time to explore gentler ways of lovemaking and new positions. Intercourse with the man on top may be painful because of pressure toward the back of the vaginal opening or at the site of an episiotomy or tear. Having the woman on top, lying side by side, or having the woman on all fours with the man behind may be more comfortable.

Women who have had cesareans find that the incision short-circuits nerve pathways, causing numbness around the scar. This numbness will disappear, for the most part, as cells regenerate. In addition to this numbing, you may find that your sexual response is altered for a few weeks. When you are reaching orgasm, the sensations may feel out of sync. This feeling will pass rapidly as your nerves repair themselves.

A common cause of discomfort during sex after childbirth is lack of vaginal lubrication. When you are sexually aroused, your body secretes substances that moisten the vagina and labia. Hormonal changes after childbirth and during breastfeeding decrease these secretions. Using a sterile vaginal lubricant on the clitoris and on the vaginal opening or the penis can help. (Do not use petroleum jelly; it does not have the necessary lubricating effect and can damage condoms.)

Breastfeeding and sex. Sexual arousal can make your milk let down and drip or spray. Don't worry about this—just keep a towel handy.

Sore nipples can, of course, interfere with sexual pleasure. Until they are healed, you'll have to forgo nipple stimulation.

Sensory overload. Something else that affects sexual desire after childbirth is sensory overload. Taking care of children is a powerful physical experience, since infants and children need close physical contact to manage in the world. A parent caring for a baby or small children all day may come to crave moments when her (or his) "personal space" isn't invaded by another human being—including a spouse.

Couples can reduce the problem of sensory overload by first recognizing it, and then arranging for the partner "on overload" to have some private time. A long, quiet, warm bath can do wonders for awakening sexual desire. A peaceful walk alone, a jog in the park, or a visit to an exercise class without children lets a person rediscover the lovely feeling of owning one's own personal space, if only for an hour or two.

Emotional overload. Intimacy extends naturally from a sense of peace with one's self and world combined with pleasure in companionship. The flowering of intimate feelings requires balance in various aspects of one's life. The early months of new parenting are a time where balance seems elusive. Suggestions from a partner about sex may be met with disbelief and insistence to "leave me alone!" Women often say, "I am just not interested in sex." Building a relationship with the baby is all-consuming work—and, like any human effort that requires total focus, it can temporarily numb sexual desire.

In the early months of parenting, many men and women worry that having a baby has ended their sex lives, or altered it so greatly that it will never be the wonderful source of pleasure and intimacy that it was before the baby was born. Like all aspects of your relationship, the sexual aspect will change—but, given time, it will be an important part of your life again. Making a successful transition through pregnancy and parenting can deepen the bond between parents. Like tempered steel, parents who have supported each other through this challenging time emerge from it stronger in their love for each other, for they are now more closely connected emotionally, spiritually, mentally, and physically.

The Madonna syndrome. Some men face a special challenge in their postpartum sexual adjustment. Their partner's new role as mother temporarily disrupts their own sense of the rightness of sexuality. This problem has been called the Madonna syndrome. The ancient taboo against sexual relations between mother and son gets confused with the idea of having sex with a mother. Men experiencing this syndrome may need to seek counseling to separate these two relationships. Continuing to call the new mother by her name rather than "Mama" or "Mommy" can help to keep relationships clearer.

Birth Control. Adequate time between pregnancies increases a woman's chances of staying healthy in a subsequent pregnancy and of having a healthy baby next time. It also gives her time to build a relationship with the baby she has.

If you decide to have intercourse before your four-or six-week postpartum checkup, it is wise to use condoms and spermicidal jelly, since some women do ovulate this soon after childbirth (especially those who aren't breastfeeding or are combining breastfeeding and bottle feeding). At the postpartum checkup you can discuss birth control options with your midwife or doctor. If you used a diaphragm or cervical cap before getting pregnant, you will need to have it refitted at this checkup, because the shape of the vagina is usually somewhat changed after a woman gives birth.

Postpartum Fathers

The Father's Feelings after Birth. Fathers who are present at birth are, more often than mothers, captured by the baby immediately. Whereas women may need minutes, hours, or a few days to feel connected to the baby, fathers often feel the power of this connection at the moment of birth. Unless the mother or baby is in some danger just after birth, the father is likely to find these moments life-changing and exquisite. These feelings are often blended with a sudden awareness of exhaustion.

A father also experiences new feelings about his mate. He may speak of his amazement at her courage, strength, and endurance during labor. He now faces the task of integrating his memory of her in labor with his previous knowledge and feelings about her.

A father may have to work through feelings he experienced while supporting the mother in labor. One of the most common feelings fathers speak about after labor is that of helplessness. Unless he is told, a man may not know how much his presence and emotional support really meant to the laboring woman.

A man may also feel that the labor experience has altered his whole life view. He may have gained a sense of the miraculous and spiritual, of a deeper meaning to life.

Not all fathers, of course, are able to share the birth experience. A lot of fathers who missed their babies' births worry that not having been there will affect their relationships with their babies. Birth is a special moment in the parent-child relationship, but it is only one moment. The years of child rearing provide many other shared moments that are just as important in the development of a relationship between father and child.

Postpartum Adjustment from the Father's Point of View. Like mothers, fathers can experience a broad range of emotions during the postpartum period, including euphoria, anxiety, detachment from the rest of the world, and the feeling that life is temporarily out of control.

After a baby's birth, fathers often have a heightened sense of their role as protector. Taking mother and baby home from the hospital may feel like transporting life that is immensely fragile. Suddenly the security of one's neighborhood or dwelling may seem terribly inadequate. Concern about being able to provide for the family may create new feelings of insecurity.

A lot of fathers speak of feeling invisible in the first weeks after birth. Visitors may greet the mother with flowers, ask how she is doing and how the labor went, then proceed to admire the baby. They may greet or congratulate the father, but rarely do they ask how he is or how he feels about the labor or the baby. In many ways, our expectations of the father's role have changed, but our support for fathers who fulfill the new, expanded role is lagging quite a bit behind. For fathers who are working hard to be involved in parenting, who feel the powerful change going on in their lives, being ignored really hurts.

A new father may be surprised at his natural ability to care for the baby in the first days. A lot of fathers will say, "I have never been any good with babies, but I just seem to know how to handle this one." This confidence can fade, however, when a father returns to work and has less time with the baby. After a few weeks, the mother's skills in caring for the baby may seem vastly superior.

A father who wants to stay involved with infant care needs to be home as much as possible and, when at home, to share responsibility for diaper changes, bathing, and comforting. It is through such tasks that parent-child relationships are built. A wise mother realizes this and gives the father a chance to learn, just as she has had to do. The baby doesn't really care if the T-shirt is on backwards or the diaper is not perfectly snug. Babies experience nurturance through touch and comfort and playful interaction, all of which will be quite different from one parent to the other. By three months of age, babies know these differences and expect them. Having two unique people to love and care for a baby benefits that child intellectually, socially, and emotionally.

During the months that follow childbirth, a father not only builds a relationship with the baby, he usually also provides critical support for the mother. A newborn demands the most of his or her primary caretaker; the baby's survival depends on the formation of this first bond. Although the father may be very involved with the baby, the first relationship is usually with the mother. A healthy mother-baby relationship develops when the mother feels nurtured. In many families, the father is the mother's only source of support and help. The care he provides her is therefore essential to the formation of the mother-baby bond.

It should not be surprising that many fathers experience the blues. Unlike the blues mothers experience a few days after birth, the blues fathers get often come much later, four or five months after birth. This may be the time a man realizes that life is not going to return to normal. It is also, however, when the attachment between mother and baby reaches a peak. Their love affair is a powerful thing to watch. A father may be pleased the baby and mother are so attached, yet he may still, understandably, feel left out and envious. Fortunately, the baby is ready to build other relationships at this age, and the involved father soon becomes a focus of the baby's attention.

Fathers *can* find support in their special role. Many communities offer classes and support groups just for fathers and their babies. Fathers who meet in childbirth classes often keep in touch with one another. It is common to see fathers in parks with their babies, creating informal support networks just as mothers have long done. Some take paternity leaves from work. Were these universally available—and if more men would take advantage of them— families would find the postpartum period an easier time by far.

Other Children in the Family

Parents having a second baby often worry how this newcomer will affect the older child. They may have two conflicting fears: first, that they will never be able to love another child as they have loved the first, and second, that they *will* love the new baby just as much. Falling in love with the second child may feel to them like infidelity to the first.

Parents often forget that having another child offers the first child the possibility of a new and rich relationship. The benefits of having a brother or sister may not be obvious to a very young child at first, or even for many years. But anyone who has strong and loving ties to a brother or sister knows that this special relationship can have a depth and openness not found in any other—including the relationship one has with parents or mate. Parents can't make such a relationship happen, of course; it has to grow of its own accord. Love is not something that can be dictated, even between siblings.

Parents having a third or later baby are usually most concerned about how the family as a whole will manage. Many say the work load is greater than they anticipated. A two-parent family, of course, has a parent for each child. With three children, there are often not enough parents to go around, even when both are home.

Larger families often thrive, though, partly because the children become an important source of learning and love for each other. In addition, children in larger families are often given more responsibilities. Unless too much is expected of them, this can help them grow up with a sense of self-importance as well as some useful skills.

Easing Children's Adjustment to the New Baby. Your older children will adjust more easily to the new baby if you have talked and read stories together about birth and new babies, if they have attended a special birth class for siblings (many hospitals offer these), and if they are familiar with the birth place. After the birth, the following ideas may help:

- Provided your children are free of any contagious disease, encourage them to visit and hold the baby as much as they like. Most birth facilities are happy to have well children visit after the birth. Screening hospital visitors is important, however, whether they are adults or children. Children who have been exposed to a communicable disease such as chicken pox should not visit, because these diseases can be spread to other families in the hospital even when symptoms are not present.
- A birthday party is something most children over the age of one understand. Offer each older child a special surprise or gift "from the baby," and have the older child bring the baby a small gift that he or she has chosen. A cupcake can serve as a birthday cake; the older child, of course, gets to eat it. This may give the child the first appreciation of the advantages of being older.
- If your children are at home while you're in the hospital or birth center, phone calls can assure them that you are available to them.
- When you come home from the hospital or birth center, have someone else carry the new baby into the house so your arms are free to greet the older children.
- While you change diapers and feed and dress the baby, encourage the older child to provide the same care to a doll or stuffed animal.
- Have your mate, a favorite friend, or a grandparent take the older children on a special outing within the first week after the baby comes. (Do this often as your children grow. Not all activities

have to involve the whole family. Each child will enjoy some special time with a parent or other beloved adult.)

- If a friend or relative is staying with you, ask this person not to try to keep your older children from you. Some will see this as protecting you, but it usually just upsets everyone.
- When another adult is holding the baby, hold your older child. Try to spend at least a few minutes each day alone with each child in your family.
- If the baby will share a room with an older child, allow for a gradual transition. Consider keeping the baby in your room for

the first several weeks. Let the older child help decide when the baby should move in to the shared room.

- Let children make some choices about which of their belongings will be given to the baby. If all of their things can be given to the baby, it is hard for children to believe that their special relationship to their parents won't be given away as well.

- Expect your children to show signs of confusion and rivalry. The first couple of weeks after the birth may be a honeymoon period between older children and their new sibling. When the older children realize that the baby is here to stay, they may say they don't want a brother or sister, or ask why you had the baby. Other signs of rivalry are sure to appear over time. These are a healthy sign that your older children are emotionally attached to you. No matter how hard you try to prevent it, the baby will seem like a threat to their relationship with you.

- Encourage your children to talk about their feelings. Mirroring these feelings—"It sounds like you are feeling angry [or lonely, or worried, or sad, or left out]"—demonstrates both respect and understanding. Don't deny that you will have less time to spend with your older children—for a while, at least. Your patient, loving responses to their concerns will show them, over time, that you continue to love them deeply and will still be able to meet their needs.

- If your children act out their feelings by hitting or pinching, help them separate the feelings from the act. Let them know it is OK to feel angry, to say one feels angry, and to show one's anger by crying or hitting a pillow or cushion. But they must understand that it is not OK to hurt the baby, or you, or themselves in any way.

  Certainly, you will not want to punish the children, either by hitting or saying things that are hurtful. This would leave them burdened with anger or hurt feelings, and possibly shame or guilt. It could also make them want even more to hurt the baby, preferably when you are not around.

- Expect young children to try acting like babies themselves. A child who was recently toilet-trained may begin to have accidents. This is why rushing a toddler through toilet training just before a sibling's birth is often a waste of time and energy. Having two children in diapers is probably easier than changing outfits because of accidents.

Weaned children will be very interested in watching you breastfeed. They may ask if they may nurse, too. If you're worried that you'll end up nursing two, you might invite the older child to sit close to you, or rest against your breast, and hear a story as you feed the baby. But if the child has long been weaned, letting him or her try nursing should do no harm.

All of these suggestions, I know, are easier said than carried out. Sibling rivalry may be normal, but it isn't much fun. You may find yourself getting upset or angry, or just plain frustrated, right along with your children. In raising my children, I found I sometimes had to take a "time-out." My spending ten minutes alone in *my* room often far surpassed the benefits of a time-out for the kids.

REFERENCES

1. National Sudden Infant Death Syndrome Clearinghouse, *What is SIDS?* (McLean, Va.: National SIDS Clearinghouse). This flyer and other resources on SIDS are available from National SIDS Clearinghouse, 8201 Greenboro Drive, Suite 600, McLean, Va. 22102. Information on SIDS is also available from the SIDS Alliance; call 800-221-SIDS.
2. Sheila Kitzinger, *The Complete Book of Pregnancy and Childbirth* (New York: Knopf, 1989), 326.
3. U. A. Hunziker and R. G. Barr, "Increased Carrying Reduces Infant Crying: A Randomized Controlled Trial," *Pediatrics* 77 (1986): 641–48.
4. T. Field *et al.*, "Massage of Preterm Newborns to Improve Growth and Development," *Pediatric Nursing* 13 (1987): 385–87.
5. Alexander Thomas, Stella Chess, *et al.*, *Behavioral Individuality in Early Childhood* (New York: New York University Press, 1963).
6. Kathleen Huggins, *The Nursing Mother's Companion*, rev. ed. (Harvard and Boston: Harvard Common Press, 1990), 128–29.
7. V. A. Beal, "Nutritional Intake," in *Human Growth and Development*, ed. R. W. Mccammon (Springfield, Ill.: Charles Thomas Publisher, 1970); and E. Grunwaldt, "The Onset of Sleeping through the Night in Infancy," *Pediatrics* 20 (1957): 556.
8. Sandy Jones, Werner Freitag, and the Editors of Consumer Reports Books, *Guide to Baby Products* (Mount Vernon, N.Y.: Consumers Union, 1989), 78.

ADDITIONAL READING

The following books may be available from your local library or bookstore. These and many other useful parenting books (and videos, too) are also available by mail-order from—

International Childbirth Education Association Bookcenter
P.O. Box 20048
Minneapolis, Minnesota 55420
To order from within the United States, call 800-624-4934
For information, call 612-854-8660

Birth and Life Bookstore
P.O. Box 70625
Seattle, Washington 98107
To order from within the United States, call 800-736-0631
For information, call 206-789-4444

Childbirth
Simkin, Penny. *The Birth Partner: Everything You Need to Know to Help a Woman through Childbirth*. Boston: Harvard Common Press, 1989.
Simkin, Penny, Janet Whalley, and Ann Keppler. *Pregnancy, Childbirth and the Newborn: The Complete Guide*. New York: Meadowbrook Press, 1991.

Breastfeeding
Huggins, Kathleen. *The Nursing Mother's Companion*, rev. ed. Boston: Harvard Common Press, 1990.

Infants and Infant Care
Klaus, Marshall H., and Phyllis H. Klaus. *The Amazing Newborn: Making the Most of the First Weeks*. Reading, Mass.: Addison-Wesley, 1985.
Shelov, Stephen, *et al.*, eds., *Caring for Your Baby and Young Child: Birth to Age Five*, New York: Bantam Books, 1991.

Parenting and Family Development
Brazelton, T. Berry. *On Becoming a Family*. New York: Delacorte Press, 1981.
Chess, Stella, and Alexander Thomas. *Know Your Child: An Authoritative Guide for Today's Parents*. New York: Basic Books, 1989.

127

For Mothers

Eagan, Andrea Boroff. *The Newborn Mother: Stages of Her Growth*. New York: Henry Holt, 1985.

Noble, Elizabeth. *Essential Exercises for the Childbearing Year: A Guide to Health and Comfort Before and After Your Baby Is Born*. Boston: Houghton Mifflin, 1988.

Siegel, Paula M. *The New Mother's Body: A Complete Guide to the First Year After Birth*. New York: Bantam Books, 1988.

For Children

Cole, Joanna. *How You Were Born*. New York: Mulberry Books, 1984.

Girard, Linda Walvoord. *You Were Born on Your Very First Birthday*. Morton Grove, Ill.: Albert Whitman, 1983.

Hoban, Russell. *A Baby Sister for Frances*. New York: Harper Trophy, 1964.

Pearse, Patricia, and Edwina Riddell. *See How You Grow*. New York: Barron's, 1988.

Loss and Grief

Borg, Susan, and Judith Lasker. *When Pregnancy Fails: Families Coping with Miscarriage, Stillbirth, and Infant Death*, rev. ed. Boston: Beacon Press, 1989.

INDEX

129